D1550883

SOUTHERN LITERARY STUDIES

Fred Hobson, Editor

A Certain Slant of Light

A Certain Slant of Light

REGIONALISM AND THE
FORM OF SOUTHERN AND
MIDWESTERN FICTION

DAVID MARION HOLMAN

With an Introduction
by
LOUIS D. RUBIN, JR.

LOUISIANA STATE UNIVERSITY PRESS
Baton Rouge and London

Copyright © 1995 by Louisiana State University Press
All rights reserved
Manufactured in the United States of America
First printing
04 03 02 01 00 99 98 97 96 95   5 4 3 2 1

Designer: Melanie O'Quinn Samaha
Typeface: Bembo
Typesetter: Impressions, a division of Edwards Bros., Inc.
Printer and binder: Thomson-Shore, Inc.

Library of Congress Cataloging-in-Publication Data

Holman, David Marion.
    A certain slant of light : regionalism and the form of southern
and midwestern fiction / David Marion Holman.
        p.   cm. — (Southern literary series)
    Includes bibliographical references and index.
    ISBN 0-8071-1870-2 (cl : alk. paper)
    1. American fiction—Southern States—History and criticism.
    2. American fiction—Middle West—History and criticism.
    3. Southern States—Intellectual life.   4. Middle West—Intellectual
    life.   5. Southern States—In literature.   6. Regionalism—Southern
    States.   7. Middle West—In literature.   8. Regionalism in
    literature.   9. Regionalism—Middle West.   I. Title.   II. Series.
    PS261.H653   1995
    813'.009'975—dc20   95-38271
                                                                              CIP

The paper in this book meets the guidelines for permanence and durability of the Committee on Production Guidelines for Book Longevity of the Council on Library Resources. ⊚

For Jo Ella and Jeff

Contents

A Certain Slant of Light

Introduction
David Marion Holman, 1951–1988

LOUIS D. RUBIN, JR.

Sometimes one must confront the human irrationality, the sense-lessness of pure, unadulterated *deprivation*. People are taken from us who have so much to offer, and every prospect of being able to offer it in distinguished fashion. It happens in war all the time, of course, but there at least the individual promise and prospects have been set aside by society for its larger ends. But on May 13, 1988, at the age of thirty-six, David Marion Holman, scholar, teacher, gentleman, dutiful son, father, husband, brother, friend, simply dropped dead of a heart attack on a golf course in Oxford, Mississippi. He left a wife, a son, a mother, a sister, an almost-completed book, and a conviction, among those who knew him, that a career as scholar in American literature that promised to be notable indeed had been, inexplicably, unconscionably, ended almost before it began.

I write this introduction, and have prepared for publication Dave Holman's book, *A Certain Slant of Light* in the Southern Literary Studies series of Louisiana State University Press, not only because I knew and admired Dave Holman and his distinguished father, C. Hugh Holman. I do so too because for several years I had been working with Dave toward the revision of what had begun as his doctoral dissertation into a book for that series, had seen it develop and take form as it moved from the enforced blandness of a document designed to satisfy the scholarly expectations of a committee of academics, into the more lively and pertinent individuality of a book meant for an anonymous reading audience. It was just about ready, lacking only a possible extension of range at the end that I should have urged Dave to undertake, when the appalling news arrived from Oxford.

In point of fact, Dave Holman's death had not come without certain advance warning. In part it was genetically forecast, in that his father had been first stricken with a heart attack while in his mid-thirties. But Hugh had recovered and, despite several other disabling attacks, had enjoyed an active career as teacher, author, and university dean and provost. Dave himself had suffered a heart attack in the late spring of 1984, shortly before he was to be married. He had come back swiftly from that, however, and from other heart complications.

Dave knew that another could strike at almost any time, that it might be fatal; he remarked to me once that he bore a genetic "silver bullet" and that he would simply have to get on with his life knowing it was there. Yet he had certainly recovered enough so that his physicians had not only allowed but had recommended that he get some exercise and that playing golf would be an excellent way to manage it. Certainly he did not expect the blow to come so soon and so savagely. When on that May day it came, it did so with such force that he was dead before he hit the ground.

A vulnerable heart, however, was not all that Dave Holman inherited from his father. C. Hugh Holman was a brilliant man; no other word will characterize the quality of his mind. He was a great teacher, a far-ranging scholar, a man who combined high intellect and impressive imagination with driving ambition and a keen grasp of practicalities. During Hugh's lifetime it was not generally known that he had made his way to the topmost rungs of the academic profession from very humble beginnings. Only after Hugh's death in early 1981 was this revealed.

Dave was enormously proud of his father, and not the least because of his ascent from just those origins. He inherited Hugh's critical acumen and his father's drive, and also possessed an excellent sense of self-humor. He could laugh at himself, see his personal experience in perspective.

David Marion Holman was born August 13, 1951, in Durham, North Carolina, to C. Hugh and Verna McLeod Holman. He was educated at Chapel Hill High School, and enrolled at Emory University, Atlanta, Georgia, in the fall of 1969, graduating with bachelor of arts degree and highest honors in humanities in 1973. At Emory he was elected to the national leadership fraternity Omicron Delta Kappa and was president of the College Council. In 1973 he began his graduate study in English literature at the University of Michigan, receiving his M.A. in 1974. After a year of doctoral study at the University of Virginia in Charlottesville, he returned to Ann Arbor in the fall of 1976 and had completed his course work and was beginning a dissertation, under the direction of Cecil Eby, when in 1979 his father suffered massive heart failure.

Whether in the hospital or at home, Hugh Holman would need continuing personal, intensive attention. Verna Holman was herself in poor health. Dave did not hesitate. He put aside his dissertation, moved back to Chapel Hill, arranged to teach part-time in the English Department where his father had taught for so many years, and for the next eighteen months he spent a major portion of his time and energy at his father's side.

It was during those years—1979 through 1981—that I came to know Dave. His father and I had been close friends, as well as coeditors of a journal and fellow academic conspirators in general. Now I came to know his son—and what a joy he was to his father! Intelligent, imaginative, well-read, a fine judge of literature, of highest integrity, and with a keen sense of humor, he made a first-class colleague.

It was a considerable satisfaction to Hugh—and to me—that Dave's literary interests had turned out to focus increasingly in precisely the area of study that his father had chosen: American literature, and in particular that of the South. Dave realized very well, of course, that in following so closely in his father's footsteps he was adding a burden to his own career that he needn't assume—that Hugh Holman was, as they say, a hard act to follow. But that was where Dave's intellectual concerns were locating themselves, and he did not back off.

Hugh died in October of 1981. The next fall Dave accepted a position as assistant professor of English at Texas A&M University. He also got back to work on his dissertation, which he completed that winter and defended in January, 1982. He also became engaged to be married to Jo Ella Walters, and the marriage was scheduled for May of 1984. Two weeks before, David suffered his first heart attack. The wedding was briefly delayed, but took place on June 1, 1984. That fall he moved on to become assistant professor of English at the University of Mississippi in Oxford. On April 27, 1986, Mr. Jefferson Marion Holman arrived on the family scene, to begin a new generation of Holmans.

I confess that it was my hope that before I retired from teaching myself, I could persuade my colleagues to bring David back to Chapel Hill permanently to join our faculty and help edit the scholarly journal his father and I had started, the *Southern Literary Journal*. Meanwhile Dave, despite developing new courses, working up an additional specialty in film, writing articles, reviews, and several subchapters in *The History of Southern Literature* (1985), a work dedicated to his father—and also experiencing other heart complications that laid him low for a time—had moved into high gear with his book.

There are two theories about writing dissertations and first books. One is to locate a very bounded and precise subject, capable of being handled tidily and with a minimum of imaginative demand, and get it done and out of the way. Needless to say, this was not Dave Holman's idea of what a dissertation or a book should be. He was not in the academic and literary business in order to avoid those topics that were important to him and that engaged his imagination. The subject he proposed, and proceeded to write on, was, in dissertation form, "A House Divided: Midwestern and Southern Literary Response to America and the American Past." For the book he rewrote it completely. The result is the present volume.

What is it about? Why, very simply, it merely takes the output of two enormously productive American regional literatures, those of the Midwest and the South, traces their evolution over the course of more than a century, and, by developing the role that history plays in the imaginations of a number of the writers involved, arrives at an extremely provocative and formidable answer to a question that has been hotly disputed by literary scholars for generations. That question is, What is "midwestern" about midwestern literature, and "southern" about southern literature, and how do they compare and contrast with each other?

It is a prodigious, demanding topic; it required for its successful completion not only the ability to read and understand literary texts as fiction, but to translate the concerns of those texts into political, social, and economic history. As book topics go, this one went a far piece indeed, ranging across the work of a dozen authors, along a north-south axis a thousand miles deep, and down more than a century of American history. It is vintage David Holman: nothing tidy and safe here, but expansive, speculative, ambitious, risk-taking.

It deserves to be published as a book, because it deals with an important comparison in an informative way, and—this is important—it shows, through example, the terms on which that comparison can profitably be developed. I think it no exaggeration to say that, implicitly, David Holman's *A Certain Slant of Light,* unfinished and unpolished though it admittedly is, offers a methodology for understanding what is *regional* in regional literature. And, considering that *all* American literature is really regional literature—if not that, then certainly the most important two-thirds of it—I submit that this constitutes quite an accomplishment for a young scholar still in his mid-thirties.

That had he lived Dave would have made this into a more polished, more finished, more inclusive work, there can be no doubt. I had urged him to conclude it by carrying his comparative methods one step further chronologically—into the reign of Hemingway, Fitzgerald, and Faulkner. As the present final chapter shows, he had begun working on that. I think I know what he would have done with it; we had talked about those writers more than once. Indeed, I was briefly tempted to try to "complete" Dave's book by adding to that last chapter, but I quickly decided against doing it. Dave's book is already a sustained unit, in the sense that it moves from the early pioneer imagination to the beginnings of twentieth-century modernism. Its scope might be extended, but what is now there is self-sufficient. And, to tack my views on the subject onto Dave's would have been an act of impertinence. He merits a hearing entirely on his own.

Here, then, is a work by a gifted scholar, who died young. It is published in its own right, for its own sake, and also to show what manner of scholar he was and what we have lost through his too-early departure. This man would have been an ornament to his profession, a maker and finder of literary study in his chosen field. He had the gift, and he had the energy and ambition to keep at work. I have taken the liberty of

inserting a dedication page, knowing full well as I do that Dave would
have placed on it precisely the names I have.

David Holman has been dead for three-and-a-half years as I write
these words; the deprivation seems as keen as ever. I think of an Irish
poet's words for a similar loss:

> I am accustomed to their lack of breath,
> But not that my dear friend's dear son,
> Our Sidney and our perfect man,
> Could share in that discourtesy of death.

Chapel Hill, North Carolina
December 1, 1991

1

Why Regionalism?

*W*hen General Robert E. Lee, Confederate States Army, and Lieutenant General Ulysses S. Grant, United States Army, met at Appomattox Court House on April 9, 1865, to discuss the terms of surrender of the Army of Northern Virginia, neither man could have fully imagined the emblematic nature of that meeting. But the event, which did not signal the surrender of all Confederate troops, has become a metaphor for the entire sectional conflict, of which the hostilities of 1861–65 were only the culmination. Paraphrasing the descriptions given by witnesses to the scene, Shelby Foote, in his narrative history of the Civil War, describes the event:

> Grant entered and went at once to Lee, who rose to meet him. They shook hands, one of middle height, slightly stooped, his hair and beard "nut-brown without a trace of gray," a little awkward and more than a little embarrassed, as he himself later said, mud-spattered trouser legs

stuffed into muddy boots, tunic rumpled and dusty, wearing no side arms, not even spurs, and the other tall and patrician-looking, immaculately groomed and clad, with his red sash and ornate sword, fire-gilt buttons and polished brass, silver hair and beard, demonstrating withal, as one observer noted, "that happy blend of dignity and courtesy so difficult to describe." Fifteen years apart in age—the younger commander's forty-third birthday was just over two weeks off—they presented a contrast in more than appearance.[1]

Grant himself, though he notes "it was not a matter that I thought of until afterwards," demonstrates in his *Personal Memoirs* that he, too, was impressed with the specific details of the encounter:

> General Lee was dressed in a full uniform which was entirely new, and was wearing a sword of considerable value, very likely the sword which had been presented by the State of Virginia; at all events, it was an entirely different sword from the one that would ordinarily be worn in the field. In my rough traveling suit, the uniform of a private with the straps of a lieutenant-general, I must have contrasted very strangely with a man so handsomely dressed, six feet high, and of faultless form.[2]

Grant's afterthought, under the scrutiny of our look backward, has become an American parable for us, just as have the first shots at Lexington and Concord and the bombing in Haymarket Square. Such events have acquired meanings of which the observers of the actual occurrence could not have conceived; they have grown from the historical into the mythological.

In the meeting of these two antagonists we have come to see the final surrender of the southern patrician to the midwestern commoner, the subjection of manners to methods, the victory of pragmatism over romanticism, the final triumph of democracy over aristocracy and slavery. As Americans, we see a prophecy of the twentieth century. But we also see more: we see regions.

A southerner or a midwesterner sees what other Americans see, but also attaches a regional importance to the event; and all of us, whatever our allegiance, can see other Americans as southerners and midwestern-

---

1. Shelby Foote, *The Civil War: A Narrative* (3 vols.; New York, 1974), III, 946.
2. *Personal Memoirs of U. S. Grant* (New York, 1886), 630.

ers, and so can participate in their regional evaluations. We expect the southerner to see in the Appomattox meeting the fall of discrete culture and its eventual replacement by industrial conformity. In the victory of the northern armies, we expect him to see the irresistible but deplorable defeat of gentlemen by a mob of commoners. Likewise, we expect the midwesterner to see Lee's surrender as a moral judgment on the degenerate aristocratic South, and the triumph of Grant's and Sherman's Army of the West, where the eastern Army of the Potomac had for so long failed to overcome its enemy, as proof that the true strength of American character and democracy resides not in the East but in the farms and small towns of the Midwest.[3] We expect this response from the southerner and the midwesterner because all of us, whether southerner, midwesterner, New Englander, or westerner, participate in a commonly held idea of region.

The concept of regionalism has often had its own political overtones that have served to obfuscate what the term *regional* really means. Frederick Jackson Turner's sectional theory of America, in which each region and its life is synecdoche for the entire country, finds its most complete application in Howard Odum's *American Regionalism: A Cultural-Historical Approach to National Integration.*[4] Professor Odum attempted in this pioneering study to define a science of regionalism for the benefit of social scientists, historians, geographers, and critics; but as is often true with critics of all disciplines, Odum's theory finally rests on a preconceived political notion of what America is, or at least ought to be. For Odum, and to a lesser degree for Turner as well, the study of region is the study of a coordinate America—a pursuit in which the regional differences ultimately point to national similarities. In *American Regionalism,* Odum declares that "the thesis of this volume is that the promise and prospect of the nation in the future is . . . to be found in the substitution of a realistic and comprehensive regionalism for the older historical sectionalism." It is his contention that "the theme of American

---

3. Sherman, in his *Memoirs of General William T. Sherman* (4th ed., 2 vols.; New York, 1875), II, 377, describes his own troops as "the most magnificent army in existence" in his account of the Grand Review in Washington. Before the march Sherman had worried that his ragtag fighting men would look ridiculous following the spit-and-polish Army of the Potomac.

4. Frederick Jackson Turner, *The Frontier in American History* (New York, 1920); Howard W. Odum and Harry Estill Moore, *American Regionalism: A Cultural-Historical Approach to National Integration* (New York, 1938).

regionalism is, after all, essentially that of a great American Nation, the land and the people, in whose continuity and unity of development, through a fine equilibrium of geographic, cultural, and historical factors must be found not only the testing grounds of American democracy but, according to many observers, the hope of western civilization."[5] It is the statement of a political idealist rather than of a social scientist.

In Odum's second chapter, "From Sectionalism to Regionalism," the discussion of regionalism becomes blurred by a semantic argument over the terms *region* and *section*. Unfortunately, that argument continues to be a pitfall in discussions of regionalism. For Frederick Jackson Turner these terms were quite useful, *region* denoting a geographical area and *section* an area of recognizable political and cultural homogeneity. *Region* refers to natural boundaries, *section* to intellectual ones. For Turner the first always composes a part of the whole, whereas the second calls attention to the differences. For Howard Odum, however, the terms become a political vocabulary; the advocate of regionalism is a nationalist, the advocate of sectionalism a separatist:

> Herein lies the essential quality of sectionalism; inherent in it is the idea of separatism and isolation; of separate units with separate interests. It must be clear that, since the very definition of regionalism implies a unifying function, it must be different from sectionalism as everywhere defined by historians. Here the distinctions are clear between the divisive power of self-seeking sections and the integrating power of co-ordinate regions fabricated into a united whole. The premise of the new regionalism goes further and assumes that the United States must not, either because of its bigness and complexity or because of conflicting interests, become a federation of conflicting sections but a homogeneity of varying regions.[6]

Odum's definitions and his political expectations for regionalism gave rise to a long-continued semantic debate over the terms *region* and *section* with Donald Davidson, a member of the Nashville Agrarian movement. Their debate, as it takes place in Odum's *American Regionalism* and Davidson's *The Attack on Leviathan,* is in actuality a dispute between a confirmed believer in national governmental centrality and an advocate of

5. Odum and Moore, *American Regionalism,* 35, 3.
6. *Ibid.,* 39.

regional political autonomy.[7] In one sense the debate is regional, in that it shows largely the divisions between Chapel Hill and Nashville political thinking; but its value to the concept of regionalism is minimal, and the damage it has done by obscuring the topic in a smoke screen of political rhetoric has been substantial.[8] Even so, I would agree that both terms, *section* and *region,* are part of the study of regionalism, and as Turner first used them to describe place and thought, they are the two truly inseparable concepts from which any idea of regionalism must proceed.

I am interested here in literary and cultural regionalism rather than in the statistical studies of geographers and social scientists. Such studies are concerned with facts; I am concerned with fictions. The facts are, of course, important to fictions, but only insofar as they help to explain the births and the fictive nature of regional mythologies. I would maintain that what is not factual, but rather what is believed without prior regard for any facts, is at the core of what informs regional mythologies and the literature of region.

Of necessity, this conception of region is dialectical. In Frederick Jackson Turner's terminology, it is both sectional and regional, because it arises simultaneously from the way a region is seen by those outside the region and the way it sees itself. Terms like *southern* and *midwestern* derive their meaning as much from the people of these regions as from those who live outside them. A regional mythology, in order to remain dynamic, must find verification of its existence outside of its region; otherwise it does not serve to delineate the region as separate and different from the rest of the country. Thus it is that Shreve McCannon can ask Quentin Compson in Faulkner's *Absalom, Absalom!,* "Why do you hate the South?" and know that he and the southern youth at least hold some common assumptions—though not common interpretations—of what the South is, that will make the question valid as communication, *as* a question.

The regional artist is always working with an awareness of this insider-

7.   Donald Davidson, *The Attack on Leviathan: Regionalism and Nationalism in the United States* (Chapel Hill, 1938).

8.   The University of North Carolina at Chapel Hill is associated through Howard W. Odum and Charles B. Aycock with the "New South" movement in southern reform. Vanderbilt University in Nashville was the seat of the "Agrarians," among whom were Tate, Ransom, Wade, Young, Davidson, Lytle, and Warren.

outsider dialectic, and it is the test of the literature that the writer is able to maintain this "we" versus "they" awareness in his work while at the same time showing that in fundamental and important ways "we" are "they" as well. Allen Tate articulates this point in his essay "The New Provincialism," in which he defines as regional the literature which, by concerning itself with the particular people and culture, and the history of its world, brings that world and its inhabitants into a true relation with those of all other worlds.[9] Thus, Tate says, "Regionalism is limited in space but not in time." Provincialism, Tate tells us, results from the concerns of a literature that has no specific significance for, or communion with, people outside the region presented.

> The provincial attitude is limited in time but not in space. When regional man, in his ignorance, often an intensive and creative ignorance, of the world, extends his own immediate necessities into the world, and assumes that the present moment is unique, he becomes provincial man. He cuts himself off from the past, and without benefit of the fund of traditional wisdom approaches the simplest problems of life as if nobody had ever heard of them before.[10]

Tate voices the thesis of most regional writers, which is that regional literature will ultimately transcend the concerns of its section, and that its focus on the particular ultimately approaches the universal.

Failure to effect a relationship between the region presented and the world outside that region results in the provincialism Tate describes in "The New Provincialism." In the opening essay of *Crumbling Idols* (1894), Hamlin Garland describes another type of provincialism, that of "feudalistic literature," which in his formulation is a literature of conformity and imitation that by its emphasis on the national or the universal ignores the particulars of culture and place that give literature substance and life.[11] Garland maintains that nonprovincial, and hence truly national, literature will be the literature of region: "It will be such a literature as no other locality could produce, a literature that could not have been written in

9. Allen Tate, "The New Provincialism," in *Essays of Four Decades* (Chicago, 1968), 535–46.
10. *Ibid.*, 539.
11. Hamlin Garland, "Provincialism," in *Crumbling Idols: Twelve Essays on Art Dealing Chiefly with Literature, Painting, and the Drama*, ed. Jane Johnson (1894; rpr. Cambridge, Mass., 1960), 10.

any other time, or among other surroundings." [12] Taken together, Tate's and Garland's differing definitions of provincialism illustrate the dilemma of many American writers. They are writing about two worlds, two countries, two cultures—that of region and that of nation. And the worlds are different, but not separate; each partakes of both. The writer must find the relationship between these worlds and the themes of his story, as, for example, Faulkner does topically in *The Town,* in which the regional social problems of modernization coalesce with the national experience. The challenge facing the regional writer is to avoid both literary myopia and hypermetropia—that is, to avoid focusing on either the unique particularity or the underlying universality of his regional world at the expense of the other.

Although a staunch defender of political sectionalism, Donald Davidson is in agreement with both Garland and Tate on the nature of literary regionalism. In an essay entitled "Regionalism and Nationalism," Davidson writes:

> We cannot define regionalism unless at the same time we define nationalism. The two are supplementary aspects of the same thing. Regionalism is a name for a condition under which the national American literature exists as a literature: that is, its constant tendency to decentralize rather than to centralize; or to correct overcentralization by conscious decentralization, or it describes the conditions under which it is possible for literature to be a normal artistic outgrowth of the life of a region.

Davidson warns that "the writer of a given region cannot shut himself away under the name 'regionalist,' but he must, from his region, confront the total and moving world." [13]

But what is a regional writer? I would define regional writers, as opposed to writers who are simply from a geographical region of the country, by the extent to which they participate in the communal psychology of the region—the extent to which their works manifest the values of the region and the extent to which those values inform the world of literature. The regional writer is writing not only

---

12.   Garland, "New Fields," in *Crumbling Idols,* 26.

13.   Donald Davidson, "Regionalism and Nationalism," in *"Still Rebels, Still Yankees" and Other Essays* (Baton Rouge, 1957), 270–71, 277.

about the region, but with an awareness gained through experience of what the region really means. The region is not merely geographical setting, but rather a nexus of values, beliefs, and customs that make it a special location for the fiction. "When we talk about a writer's country," Flannery O'Connor remarks,

> we are liable to forget that no matter what particular country it is, it is inside as well as outside of him. Art requires a delicate adjustment of the outer and inner worlds in such a way that, without changing their nature, they can be seen through each other. To know oneself is to know one's region. It is to know the world, and it is also, paradoxically, a form of exile from that world. The writer's value is lost, both to himself and to his country, as soon as he ceases to see that country as a part of himself.[14]

The regional artist is participant in as well as reporter on the region and, as arbiter of the worlds outside of and within the region, fully participates in both. Harriet Beecher Stowe's New England is richer than her South of *Uncle Tom's Cabin;* it is a more complete and complex world, and finally a more recognizable one.

Few writers set out to be "regional." Indeed, "regional writer" is an appellation that is apt to meet with scorn from writers themselves, if not from critics. The term implies local color as the writer's predominant aim. Few southern writers would appreciate being grouped with Thomas Nelson Page, and few midwestern writers with Edward Eggleston. Certainly this aversion has to do not only with artistic quality—although it may be more so with Page than with Eggleston—but also with authorial intention in the creation of a literary work. Local color, as the examination and presentation of exotics, is anathema to the aims of most serious writers to present not only a region but the world as they see it. As O'Connor remarks, the novelist is presenting the world within as well as without. Local color is concerned mainly with the outside world—its surfaces.

This is not to say that the writer always abjures the title "regional," only that he does so when it is used as an indicator of limitation. The artist wants to be considered in the main group, "writers," before he is

---

14. Flannery O'Connor, "The Fiction Writer & His Country," in *Mystery and Manners,* ed. Sally Fitzgerald and Robert Fitzgerald (New York, 1969), 34–35.

placed as well into the subset "regional writer." The rationale behind this feeling is clear; one wants to be a large fish in the largest possible pond. Just as Ralph Ellison balked at being labeled one of the best black authors, so William Faulkner would have been nonplussed at being pronounced "one of the best Mississippi writers," or best southern writers, for that matter. *Regional* is often the faint praise that damns.

Yet *regional,* as I employ it in this investigation of American writers, is *not* a limiting term but rather a method of explaining, in part, the cultural consciousness that lies behind and indeed informs the literary achievement of many distinguished American authors. To speak of American literature or of anything "American" necessarily implies that there is somewhere a recognizable America, or in the case of literature, a recognizable American tradition. To speak of regional literature, or indeed of region, seems to imply that, in truth, this single America never exists. What is regional about American literature eludes social scientific quantification, at least for the twentieth-century American. To the observer who knew nothing of the country before he visited, the noticeable differences would appear to be economic—industrial and agricultural and social—rural and urban. Yet as that observer traveled throughout the country, he would find regional differences in the cultures, attitudes, and life-styles of the peoples of different areas. If he lived long enough in the various parts of the nation, he would be likely to generalize less about "Americans" and more about southerners, New Englanders, midwesterners, westerners, and, today, Californians. He would come finally to the conclusion that there is in fact both one America and, simultaneously, several Americas.[15] He would also conclude that the existence of these several Americas could not be explained simply by settlement patterns, climate, income, and per capita tabulations of bourbon or Scotch consumed or churches attended, although each of these figures would perhaps be useful to his investigation. He could not explain through these quantifiers the difference in attitudes of a Boston millionaire, an Atlanta millionaire, a Dallas millionaire, and a Chicago millionaire, although they might help to explain the differences in the ways that these four came to

15. If this hypothetical observer remained long enough in the South, he would come to see that there are many Souths as well, just as he would find multiple divisions within any southern state; but he also would see, I think, that the divisions between those Souths are not as radical as the divisions between the South and the rest of the United States.

be millionaires. And it is likely that he would find these four urban gentlemen more nearly similar in attitudes than three farmers from Michigan, South Carolina, and New Hampshire, or three insurance salesmen from Cartersville, Georgia; Lancaster, Vermont; and Carbondale, Illinois. If he stayed long enough in each region, he might even be able to delineate the different personalities of each communal psychology and also to articulate the similarities. But in order to account for these cultural differences, he would have to discuss the regional mythologies that underlie them. Again, he would have to differentiate between the regional and national mythologies; in doing so, he would find that America is a country of both shared and unshared pasts.

The shared, or national, past would include such events as George Washington's apocryphal tossing of the dollar across the Potomac River or the united stand of the colonies in the meetings of the Continental Congress. He would find across the country a general shared reverence for the Founding Fathers, for Thomas Jefferson, and for Benjamin Franklin. He would find eventually, however, that in historical events such as the meeting of Grant and Lee at Appomattox the shared past divides into unshared regional interpretations. And it is through his examination of these different historical mythologies that he would find the mythological frameworks that underlie the regional psychologies he has witnessed. He would find, in fact, that Lee's surrender was contemporary with the development of the regional mind that he encountered.

In this investigation I will concentrate upon selected midwestern and southern writers whose works appeared between 1832 and 1925, the year in which *The Great Gatsby* was published and fictional modernism became a major force in American letters. My reasons for selecting these two regions are fourfold. The first and most obvious reason, because this is a literary investigation of regionalism, is that the South and the Midwest have generated the largest number of writers who have made the most significant contributions to modern American fiction. Certainly from World War I on, Americans from all the regions of the country have produced important and enduring fiction, but an overwhelming number of these writers have come out of the South and the Midwest: Glasgow, Faulkner, Wolfe, Tate, O'Connor, Warren, Caldwell, Welty, and Percy from the South; and midwesterners Cather, Anderson, Lewis, Fitzgerald, and Hemingway (particularly in the Nick Adams stories). That the fiction of these two regions, until the third decade of the twentieth century, is characterized by the use of two distinct fictional modes—romance in the South and social realism in the Midwest—is also of great interest.

A second reason for selecting the South and the Midwest for this study is that, largely because of the Civil War, the South is the section most easily defined and accepted by the nation *as* region, whereas the Midwest is the region that defines itself most as nation and is accepted as such by other regions of the country. The South is a particular *place;* the Midwest is "the Heartland." Even today the southerner is recognizable nationally by accent and by vernacular; the South is still the most rural region of the country. The Midwest also has less identification with specific historical events such as the Civil War, the founding of the Plymouth Colony, or the Gold Rush than do other sections of the country. Its great industrial and metropolitan centers and its abundant farmlands as well contribute to the national and regional conception of the Midwest as microcosm of the national macrocosm.

Third, the South and the Midwest are more than a century and a half apart in their settlement and their cultural development, and hence are historically different regions. Both have distinct regional "minds," to use W. J. Cash's term; and yet, at the basis of these minds, each has an agrarian philosophy that even today continues as a strong cultural influence.

Finally, in their attitudes toward their pasts, the mythologies of these two regions are diametrically opposed. The past of the South is tragic and complete, and the present and the future are measured by the idea of the Lost Cause. The midwestern mind is characterized by its belief in the possibility that the promise of the past can be realized in the future, and the present is thus a constant reminder of the region's and the nation's failure to keep faith with the ideals of the past and with the promise of the future.

None of these four hypotheses is exclusive of the others—at least not for the investigation of literature. My descriptions and conclusions about the development of social realism in the Midwest and of the romance form in the South, and then the turning away from those forms, rest finally on a belief that the literature of a region, both in form and in content, is inseparable from the culture in which that literature is written. It is my assumption, too, that literature is no mere cultural artifact, but a dynamic force that can affect as well as be affected by the culture in which it is produced.

As I have sought to show earlier, we can discern multiple regional meanings in a single historical event—Lee's surrender at Appomattox, for example. It is those meanings, and the minds that construct them, that ultimately provide the materials for the regional writer. The great events in the myth-making minds of the South and the Midwest, respectively, are the Civil War and the settling of the Middle States—the myth of the aristocrat and the myth of the pioneer. Consider the two following passages, which are perhaps epigrammatic for these regional attitudes. The first is from William Faulkner's *Intruder in the Dust:*

> For every Southern boy fourteen years old, not once but whenever he wants it, there is the instant when it's still not yet two oclock on that July afternoon in 1863, the brigades are in position behind the rail fence, the guns are laid and ready in the woods and the furled flags are already loosened to break out and Pickett himself with his long oiled ringlets and his hat in one hand probably and his sword in the other looking up the hill waiting for Longstreet to give the word and it's all in the balance, it hasn't happened yet, it hasn't even begun yet, it not only hasn't begun yet but there is still time for it not to begin against that position and those circumstances which made more men than Garnett and Kemper and Armstead and Wilcox look grave yet it's going to begin, we all know that, we have come too far with too much at stake and that moment doesn't need even a fourteen-year-old boy to think *This time. Maybe this time* with all this much to lose and all this much to gain.[16]

The second is from Louis Bromfield's *The Green Bay Tree:*

> Besides, life is hard for our children, Hattie. It isn't as simple as it was for us. Their grandfathers were pioneers and the same blood runs in their veins, only they haven't a frontier any longer. They stand . . . these children of ours . . . with their backs toward this rough-hewn middle west and their faces set toward Europe and the East. And they belong to neither. They are lost somewhere between.[17]

---

16. William Faulkner, *Intruder in the Dust* (New York, 1948), 194–95.
17. Louis Bromfield, *The Green Bay Tree* (New York, 1924), 107.

About the actual causes of the Civil War little needs to be said here except to repeat that this conflict, like so many others, was at least as much one of economics and politics, specifically of tariff laws and congressional balance, as it was a moral conflict over slavery or a class system. What is important, however, to the southern mind is precisely that belief in the existence of a culture of chivalry, in the inherent honor of the Lost Cause, and yet also a recognition of the tragedy of slavery. As Faulkner's passage shows, it is belief that is important—in the completeness of the past, in a cause lost, and so finished, completed, and therefore meaningful, comprehensible, and mythic. In *Jefferson Davis Gets His Citizenship Back,* Robert Penn Warren emphasizes this completeness, adding that "it was not until Appomattox that the conception of Southern identity truly bloomed—a mystical conception, vague but bright, floating high beyond the criticism of brutal circumstances."[18]

Perhaps the Midwest, as a less often discussed region, needs more explanation. The midwesterner inherits the myth of the farmer and pioneer. Like the characters of Willa Cather's *My Ántonia* or O. E. Rölvaag's *Giants in the Earth,* the midwesterner comes out of the East, the world's melting pot, looking for something better, and finds it in the land that blossoms from the sweat of his brow. Here are the true people of Carl Sandburg's *The People, Yes;* here is America, the bastion of democratic values, the Heartland, the home of simple, moral folk. This is the myth— the Kansas of *The Wizard of Oz.*

These are the facts: by 1850, 70 percent of the Midwest's population lived in towns or cities larger than fifteen hundred people. By 1880, less than half the midwestern families who engaged in farming owned the land they farmed. In Iowa, for example, twenty-seven million of the thirty-six million acres of farmland passed through the hands of land speculators. And presently in the Midwest, the city population outnumbers the rural population by better than two to one.[19]

Yet it is the myth that is important.

The regional writer is writing in response to these mythologies, and often in reaction to them. Although the southern writer and the mid-

---

18. Robert Penn Warren, *Jefferson Davis Gets His Citizenship Back* (Lexington, Ky., 1980), 59.

19. Paul Sharp, "From Poverty to Prosperity," in *The Heritage of the Middle West,* ed. John J. Murray (Norman, Okla., 1958), 54–72; Ray Allen Billington, "The Garden of the World: Fact and Fiction," *ibid.,* 27–53; John D. Hicks, "A Political Whirlpool," *ibid.,* 73–96.

western writer are both Americans, they are responding to different American pasts. For the southerner that past is both heritage and trap, as exemplified in Faulkner, Glasgow, Welty, and Wolfe. Like the Twelve Southerners who took their stand in 1930, the southern writer must simultaneously use and reconstruct the past.[20] With notable exceptions— Erskine Caldwell, for instance—the element of a gothic past lies just beneath the surface of most southern writing. Even so realistic a novel as Ellen Glasgow's *Barren Ground* cannot escape the ravages of a romantic past; the reader senses, beneath Glasgow's examination of southern class structure, resonances of chains rattling in the slave quarters or the moonlit scene of a woman in a white dress running to or from an imposing plantation house. Even in writing about the present, the southern writer must confront, directly or indirectly, the ghosts of the past—ghosts that may be exorcised, vilified, satirized, or romanticized, but not ignored.

But if the southern past, the Lost Cause, is one of mythic and, to use Tate's adjective, "immoderate" completion, the midwestern past is one of promise unfulfilled and unattained.[21] It is a past that is attractive to the midwestern writer only at a distance—attractive to Nick Carraway only after he has seen New York, to *My Ántonia's* Jim Burden and *Winesburg, Ohio's* George Willard only after they have left for the city. Midwesterners flee the Midwest, voyaging to the East and to Europe. As Craig Watson has remarked, if the southerner says, "I'll take my stand," the midwest-erner proclaims, "I'll take my flight—preferably the first one out."[22] For those midwesterners who stay, the promise of the past and its perversion in the present must be confronted, and the dominant mode of this con-frontation is realism. Where the southerners—Faulkner, Caldwell, O'Connor, Welty, and McCullers—are storytellers, the midwesterners— Sherwood Anderson, Sinclair Lewis, Floyd Dell, and Bromfield—are lec-turers. Midwestern literary humor is satire; southern humor is distanc-

20. Twelve Southerners, *I'll Take My Stand: The South and the Agrarian Tradition* (New York, 1930). The Twelve Southerners were John Crowe Ransom, Donald Davidson, Frank L. Owsley, John Gould Fletcher, Lyle H. Lanier, Allen Tate, Herman Clarence Nixon, Andrew Lytle, Robert Penn Warren, John Donald Wade, Henry Blue Kline, and Stark Young.

21. Allen Tate, "Ode to the Confederate Dead," in *Collected Poems, 1919–1976* (New York, 1977), 21.

22. Craig Watson, "I'll Take My Flight: The Village Lost and Found," in "Habit of Mind: Studies in the Literature of the Middle West of the Twentieth Century" (Ph.D. dissertation, University of Michigan, 1980).

ing—black humor, the grotesque. The difference can be seen clearly in the bedchamber of Faulkner's "A Rose for Emily" and the dining room of Cather's "Sculptor's Funeral."

Both southerner and midwesterner confront a modern America that is bleak in comparison with their historical pasts. But the definition of that disparity between past and present is different for each region. For the inheritor of the pioneer legacy, the world is now too confining, too organized, too conformist. For the southerner, the world is in chaos, lacking the organization and order once present in manners and a defined class structure. In one sense these writers are confronting the same America, but it is an America made different for each region by a different and unshared mythological past.

Ultimately these two Americas, the shared national America and the unshared regional America, lie not in the present but in the past—not a historical past but a mythological one. America has always been a future-oriented country, but one obsessed with the past and the creation of a past for itself. The post–Revolutionary War American of the late eighteenth century, lacking a past by virtue of having spurned Europe, found himself uniquely contemporary with the mythologies he created. In numerous statues and paintings, Revolutionary War heroes and statesmen were portrayed in classical garb, and even as classical gods. The euphuistic was embodied in the literal, so that many almost believed George Washington to merit not only figuratively but literally the Zeus-like attribute "Father of the Country." America became nationally what North America had been figuratively—the New Eden. As a nation with a future, America had to seize upon a past. In a matter of years, "the shot heard 'round the world" had achieved the status of archetype.

The call for an American literature that had been voiced by Charles Brockden Brown, Thomas Jefferson, Washington Irving, William Gilmore Simms, Ralph Waldo Emerson, Walt Whitman, and others was not a call for literature about things indigenous, but for a literature communicated by a mind indigenous, and in the years after the turn of the twentieth century young American critics attempted to aid in calling that literature into being. As Richard Ruland notes, the past was the idiom for that call.[23] In an essay entitled "On Creating a Usable Past," which

23. Richard Ruland, *The Rediscovery of American Literature: Premises of Critical Taste, 1900–1940* (Cambridge, Mass., 1967), 5.

appeared in the April 11, 1918, issue of *The Dial,* Van Wyck Brooks laments that "the American writer . . . not only has the most meager of birthrights but is cheated out of that." Brooks continues, "The present is a void, and the American writer floats in that void because the past that survives in the common mind of the present is a past without living value." "If we need another past so badly," he exhorts, "is it inconceivable that we might discover one, that we might even invent one?"[24]

Yet by 1918 the past was not only usable but used, even though fundamentally unshared by the regions that compose America. To Brooks and others, the gaping holes in the shared American mythology clearly exhibited the regional differences. Brooks was correct in his assertion that the "spiritual past has no objective reality; it yields only what we are able to look for in it"; but in 1918, and even today, Americans were not and are not looking for the same things.[25] At the time of Brooks's call to arms, many western territories had been open for barely half a century, whereas New England and the seaboard South had been settled for over two hundred fifty years. What the different regions of the country shared was less than the differences they reflected.

The search to articulate an "American Tradition" in literature, an undertaking admirably explored and explained by Howard Mumford Jones in *The Theory of American Literature,* has always had at its core the belief that what is shared in the American mythological past is of greater importance than the sum of the component mythologies of America's regions.[26] This search for an American Tradition, which finds its most virile progenitors in Emerson and Whitman, has elevated the academic study of American letters from a single professorship before 1917 to a growing and respected academic field in the American and international academies. It has also, in the last quarter-century, driven American literature scholars to yield, in despair of arriving at a comprehensive American picture, to the employment of narrowly focused theoretical methods, or else to try to make a more manageable picture out of American letters by forcing the literature into a molded thesis rather than by shaping the thesis to the literature. The latter impulse has resulted in intelligent and

24.   Van Wyck Brooks, "On Creating a Usable Past," *The Dial,* April 11, 1918, pp. 337–41.
25.   *Ibid.,* 338.
26.   Howard Mumford Jones, *The Theory of American Literature* (Ithaca, 1948).

provocative but nevertheless oversimplified thesis books such as R. W. B. Lewis' *The American Adam* and Leo Marx's *The Machine in the Garden.*[27]

The myth of the Garden, the New Eden, as espoused by Lewis, Marx, Henry Nash Smith, and others, is a dynamic idea of the American frontier and its settlement.[28] It is descriptive both of the political hopes of the American settler and of the landscapes he encountered, and is an image voiced, for different reasons, by Captain John Smith of Virginia and by the Puritan settlers in New England. Yet this conformity is misleading; the New Eden as idea results more from a basic European Christian orientation and education—later the idea will be that of Prometheus—than from a unity of ideals and experiences. The New England settlers and the southern settlers, and later the western settlers, all encountered metaphorical gardens in America, but those gardens were as dissimilar as a tropical greenhouse and an Oriental rock-sage arrangement.

When the settlers at Jamestown eyed the green, rolling Virginia coastline and the settlers at Plymouth viewed the rocky New England coast, and both proclaimed "Garden," the lack of communication between the two groups was almost total. The garden that met the eye and the garden that met the mind's eye were as radically dissimilar as the attitudes and beliefs that had brought the appellation "Eden" to each group's mind in the first place. Purposes differing, so did the gardens seen. Both gardens were edenic and economic, but at Jamestown, Eden was in the service of economy; at Plymouth, economy was at the service of Eden.

The American Tradition is often concerned more with the similar manifestations of the Garden than with the differences that the gardens present. Thus the American Studies approach that links Puritan intellectual thought with Jeffersonian politics often leaves gaping blank spaces in the American "big picture." That the South and New England existed together under the rubric "democracy" can only reveal that the term had for Americans, as it has throughout political history, different meanings. That the descendants of Plymouth and Jamestown could subscribe

---

27. R. W. B. Lewis, *The American Adam: Innocence, Tragedy, and Tradition in the Nineteenth Century* (Chicago, 1955); Leo Marx, *The Machine in the Garden: Technology and the Pastoral Ideal in America* (New York, 1964).

28. Henry Nash Smith, *Virgin Land: The American West as Symbol and Myth* (Cambridge, Mass., 1950).

together to the litany "life, liberty, and the pursuit of happiness" indicates that the terms were large enough to accommodate often radically different opinions of what these terms meant, and were also abstract enough to avoid an immediate confrontation over those differences.

Even today, with the almost total destruction of indigenous folklore by mass media culture and with the uniformity of local economics brought about by technological advances and national and multinational corporations, Americans still recognize America as a confederation of regions and regional attitudes. Accessible transportation has not removed the exoticism of place. At no time is region more prominent than in the selection of a political party's candidate for president, in which to be considered viable, the candidate must be able to win primaries in regional blocks—the Midwest, New England, the West, and the South.

That a country the size of Central Europe should be a country of marked regional differences is not surprising. In fact, the American traveler is often as surprised to hear a generalization about "Americans" as a Frenchman would be to hear himself included in a remark about Europeans. Certainly, to speak of America is to speak of a people politically, socially, and economically more homogeneous than the people of the Common Market. Yet Van Wyck Brooks's call for a "usable past" was a recognition that the shared American past was indeed barely strong enough to sustain an American Tradition in letters.

The problem was, of course, one for critics, teachers, social scientists—those who were asked or felt compelled to present a unified American Tradition. Writers had found a past that was usable, rich, and varied, and many of them found and no doubt will continue to find in their regions the unshared mythological pasts—the communal consciousness that frames and informs their works and that makes the events in our shared history, such as Grant's meeting with Lee at Appomattox Court House, resonate with new meanings.

2

Regionalism and Romance: Cooper, Hawthorne, and Simms

*I*nsofar as the national letters are concerned, the southern–midwest-ern equation is a post–Civil War phenomenon. Prior to 1860 there was one great story for the American writer to tell: the settlement of the frontier and the subsequent development of American society—what Charles Olson has labeled "the history of the last first people in the world."[1] It was a story begun in the journals of John Smith and Sir Walter Raleigh, and referred to by Shakespeare in *The Tempest*. It was the ad-venture that fascinated Tocqueville, Chateaubriand, Crèvecoeur, and others. It was the story undertaken by three of America's best romancers: James Fenimore Cooper, Nathaniel Hawthorne, and William Gilmore Simms. The first two were easterners, the third a southerner. When after

---

1. Charles Olson, *Call Me Ishmael* (New York, 1947), 14.

the Civil War the voice of the Midwest began to be heard in literature, it would be in opposition to all three. But to understand that midwestern voice we must first look at what was being written before it materialized. By contrast, the South had begun articulating its presence early on, and what it had to say thereafter was significantly shaped by its separate states as a region.

As writers, Cooper, Hawthorne, and Simms share much in common. All three wrote frontier and Revolutionary War fiction. All were theorists of as well as practitioners of the romance form. All were strong proponents for the recognition of American literature. Yet to read the Leatherstocking Tales, *The Scarlet Letter,* and *The Yemassee* is to experience the frontiers of three different Americas—places that are vastly different in climate, geography, social organization, and, of most importance, in the values and concerns of the people. To read these novels is to experience America as nation, America as New England, and America as the South.

In *Notions of the Americans* (1828), Cooper voiced his famous complaint about the plight of the American writer of his day:

> There is scarcely an ore which contributes to the wealth of the author, that is found, here, in veins as rich as in Europe. There are no annals for the historian; no follies (beyond the most vulgar and commonplace) for the satirist; no manners for the dramatist; no obscure fictions for the writer of romance; no gross and hardy offences against decorum for the moralist; nor any of the rich artificial auxiliaries of poetry. . . . I have never seen a nation so much alike in my life, as the people of the United States, and what is more, they are not only like each other, but they are remarkably like that which common sense tells them they ought to resemble. . . .
>
> All attempts to blend history with romance in America, have been comparatively failures, (and perhaps fortunately,) since the subjects are too familiar to be treated with the freedom that the imagination absolutely requires.[2]

The views expressed sound remarkably similar to the position Van Wyck Brooks later articulated in "On Creating a Usable Past." Three decades after Cooper, in his preface to *The Marble Faun* (1860), Hawthorne makes a similarly famous complaint:

2. James Fenimore Cooper, *Notions of the Americans: Picked up by a Travelling Bachelor* (2 vols.; Philadelphia, 1828), II, 108, 111–12.

No author, without a trial, can conceive of the difficulty of writing a Romance about a country where there is no shadow, no antiquity, no mystery, no picturesque and gloomy wrong, nor anything but a commonplace prosperity, in broad and simple daylight, as is happily the case with my dear native land. It will be very long, I trust, before romance-writers may find congenial and easily handled themes either in the annals of our stalwart Republic, or in any characteristic and probable events of our individual lives. Romance and poetry, like ivy, lichens, and wall-flowers, need Ruin to make them grow.[3]

William Gilmore Simms, however, found no lack of mystery, legends, annals, and "ruin"—the stuff of which, according to Cooper and Hawthorne, romance is made. Simms voices no complaint about his materials. In fact, Vernon Parrington criticizes Simms for his prodigality of invention; of Simms's best-known novel, *The Yemassee* (1835), Parrington remarks, "A wealth of romantic material is crowded into the volume, enough to serve Cooper for half a dozen tales."[4]

In view of the contributions of Cooper and Hawthorne to the development of an indigenous American literature, no matter how familiar these two writers' disparagements of their native materials may be, it is nevertheless hard for a modern reader to believe these dyspeptic invectives as anything more than the obligatory self-deprecations of a "Humble Servant" addressing his "Dear Reader." Yet why are such remarks not to be found in the prefaces of Simms?

The answer, in part, may be found in Simms's dedication to the 1856 edition of his *The Wigwam and the Cabin:*

One word for the material of these legends. It is local, sectional—and to be *national* in literature, one must needs be *sectional*. No one mind can fully or fairly illustrate the characteristics of any great country; and he who shall depict *one section* faithfully, has made his proper and sufficient contribution to the great work of *national* illustration.[5]

3. Nathaniel Hawthorne, preface to *The Marble Faun; or, The Romance of Monte Beni,* ed. William Charvat et al. (Columbus, Ohio, 1968), 3, Vol. IV of *The Centenary Edition of the Works of Nathaniel Hawthorne.*

4. Vernon Louis Parrington, Jr., *The Romantic Revolution in America* (New York, 1958), 135, Vol. II of Parrington, *Main Currents in American Thought: An Interpretation of American Literature from the Beginnings to 1920.*

5. William Gilmore Simms, *The Wigwam and the Cabin* (New York, 1882), 4.

Simms's contention here that American literature is the aggregate of regional literatures sets him apart in the theory of American literature. The
insistence on America as a collection of regions voices a theory of sectional literature that would find its most complete expression forty years
later in Hamlin Garland's regional literary manifesto *Crumbling Idols*
(1894).[6] What is most important to note here is that Simms's South could
apparently provide him with a wealth of materials that Hawthorne and
Cooper found insufficiently available in their attempts to describe a
nation.

Certainly Simms, Hawthorne, and (in some ways) Cooper were all
regional writers, and certainly all aspired to be national writers as well.
Yet of the three, only Simms equated being a national writer *with* being
a regional one. In doing so, he could make use of regional differences as
well as national similarities and therefore always had before him a wealth
of materials he found usable for romantic fiction.

It is Cooper's insistence on Americans as a single people in a single
society that leads him finally to his statement, "I have never seen a nation
so much alike in my life, as the people of the United States." In *Rob Roy,*
for example, Cooper's literary idol, Sir Walter Scott, could draw multiple
distinctions between highlanders, midlanders, and lowlanders. In America, a century before Cooper, William Byrd could delineate differences
between North Carolinians and Virginians. But Cooper's main distinctions are finally made between whites and Indians—native red men and
European-Americans.

I do not mean that Cooper was insensitive to regional distinctions; as
novels of manners his Satanstoe trilogy, for example, minutely describes
his New York culture. Rather, it is as a writer of historical romance that
Cooper's demand for American archetypes for the American frontier
story leads him to his complaint about his materials. For Cooper it is not
so much the richness of the "ore," as he states in his 1828 complaint, but
rather a question of the quantity of that ore available for the particular
form of romance he wants to write. Viewed as a single culture, America
must have seemed a weak mine indeed; looking for El Dorado, he saw
few nuggets worthy of his attention.

6.   Hamlin Garland, *Crumbling Idols: Twelve Essays on Art Dealing Chiefly with Literature, Painting,
and the Drama* ed. Jane Johnson (1894; rpr. Cambridge, Mass., 1960).

In one sense the wilderness, the setting for most of the action of the Leatherstocking novels, is precisely the place where America is *not,* and when that setting becomes the frontier settlement and hence no longer a wilderness, Cooper, like Natty Bumppo, moves on. Like his woodsman, Cooper is at his weakest in the settlements. Throughout the Leatherstocking saga, and especially in *The Pioneers,* Cooper attempts to people his novels with a cross-section of white Americans; but these men and women are differentiated more by accent than by differences in culture, and except for vicissitudes of moral character are readily distinguishable mainly as whites or non-Indians. In Cooper's novels we see the American Frontier Story played out by archetypes, noble savages and heroic woodsmen doomed by the very encroachment of civilization that Cooper as romancer laments and as New Yorker lauds.

If Cooper's frontier romances seem more generalized than those of Hawthorne or Simms, the reason may be attributed to the form of romance that Cooper was attempting and the views of history that that form implies. Cooper often voices his debts to Sir Walter Scott, and the Leatherstocking Tales, like Scott's Waverley novels, are more concerned with the effects of historical forces upon the characters of the romance than with the effect of the characters upon history. Like Scott, Cooper chooses for his novels a time in which an old order is giving way to a new one—in the Leatherstocking Tales, the time when the wilderness is giving way to the settlements. Like Scott's heroes, Natty Bumppo is caught between two worlds—that of the pioneer and that of the settler. Rather than ultimately influencing that world, he is finally doomed by it. He is a man caught out of place between the world of the Indian, which preceded him, and the world of the frontier settlement, which succeeds him. Like Scott's heroes and heroines, Leatherstocking is the victim of historical progression rather than the author of it.

But unlike Scott's novels, Natty Bumppo's story does not finally take place in one specific place in one specific time, but rather in a progression of times, from the 1740s to the 1800s, and a progression of places, from the woods of upstate New York to the midwestern prairies. The dilemma facing Cooper as romancer was quite different from any problem Scott encountered. Where Scott could select a specific national event, Cooper had to find a regional one and try to nationalize it. The events of Scott's novels are played out in a completed past; the events of Cooper's Leath-

erstocking saga were the past only for one region. The story of the
frontier, though completed in New York, was still taking place farther
west. The opening of the Iowa territory in 1833 coincided with the
midpoint of Cooper's authorship of the five novels. And the national
story continued to the settlement of California and its admission to the
Union in 1850, and then back eastward to the Oklahoma land rush of
1889.

Scott could draw upon a completed past and situate his novels at the
moments when historical and philosophical forces coalesced. Cooper
found himself confronted with a nation's history of rapid linear expan-
sion, one that was still going on. The historical theories of Scott, the
stories of the historical character doomed by the conflict of historical
forces in the moment, were finally unavailable to Cooper. Natty's kind
was not ultimately doomed until the twentieth century, and thus he had
the option that Scott's theory and form did not allow—he could run
until the moment exhausted him, but not until he exhausted the moment.[7]

When Cooper wrote in 1828 that "all attempts to blend history with
romance in America have been comparatively failures," the comparison
was with the historical romance as practiced by Scott. The "failure" of
Cooper's Leatherstocking Tales—and indeed the implication of failure is
relative only to what Cooper wanted to accomplish and not to the enduring work he produced—lies in the inadequacy of the form he wanted
to use to tell the story he wanted to tell. Cooper's allegiance to the
Scottian romance and its theory of historical forces, and the uniquely
American situation Cooper confronted in a national history that was
completing itself not over time but over distance, perhaps explain why
Cooper felt compelled to deprecate the romantic materials available to
him. If, as modern readers, we are puzzled now by Cooper's self-
condemnation, it is because the story Cooper wanted to tell has been
completed for us in the past, whereas for Cooper it was incomplete.

Cooper was the only major writer to attempt to work out the Scottian

---

7. The Leatherstocking novels were not written in a chronological order for Natty Bumppo's
age. The publication date of *The Prairie*, which contains Leatherstocking's death, was 1827. Cooper
revived his scout in *The Pathfinder* (1840) and *The Deerslayer* (1841). When Bumppo dies, the Midwest
is still wilderness; when Cooper tells the two later stories of Bumppo's youth, the Midwest is
becoming settled at a rapid rate.

romance on a consciously national scale; Simms and Hawthorne, in their best work, are distinctly regional romancers. Like Simms, Hawthorne found in his region the history, manners, and obscure fictions that Cooper claimed eluded his nation. *The Scarlet Letter* (1850) and *The House of the Seven Gables* (1860) are stories of New England, its society and history. Hawthorne's original, unpublished collection of stories was to have been entitled *Seven Tales of My Native Land* and was to contain exclusively New England stories. Like Simms, Hawthorne, as romancer, found the histories and legends of his region to be rich in material.

As C. Hugh Holman has pointed out, Hawthorne and Simms were adamant in their insistence on the separation of the romance and the novel as descriptions of fictional forms, and both were strikingly similar in their definitions of that separation.[8] Simms, in his preface to the 1853 edition of *The Yemassee,* and Hawthorne, in his preface to *The House of the Seven Gables,* both firmly distinguish between the realism and fidelity to probability required by the novel and the licenses of history and legend permitted by the romance. Though Hawthorne shows little of Simms's "epic" impulse in his fiction, Simms would certainly agree with Hawthorne's contention about the romance:

> The point of view in which this Tale comes under the Romantic definition, lies in the attempt to connect a by-gone time with the very Present that is flitting away from us. It is a Legend, prolonging itself, from an epoch now gray in the distance, down into our own broad daylight, and bringing along with it some of its legendary mist.[9]

To read Hawthorne and Simms is to see the use that each writer makes of a completed regional past and how that past is projected in the regional mind of the present. Certainly most historical fiction is as much about the time in which it is written as it is about the time in which the action of the story takes place. The past that the writer presents, or more specifically the attitude of the author toward the past as he depicts it, is a

8. C. Hugh Holman, introduction to *The Yemassee,* by William Gilmore Simms (Boston, 1961), xv–xvi.

9. Nathaniel Hawthorne, *The House of the Seven Gables,* ed. William Charvat, Roy Harvey Pearce, and Claude M. Simpson (Columbus, Ohio, 1965), 2, Vol. II of *The Centenary Edition of the Works of Nathaniel Hawthorne.*

product of the present that the author experiences. It is not so much history as it is history made meaningful.

It is not surprising, then, that Simms, in his fictional accounts of South Carolina history, particularly in *The Partisan* (1835), *Mellichampe* (1836), and *The Scout* (1841), shows the American Revolution as a class struggle in which the American heroes are generally the patrician upper-class farmers, and the mercenary loyalists are lower-class whites and immigrants of non-British background. The conflicts of Simms's Revolution are the same conflicts of the South in the 1830s and 1840s, and those that ultimately would be the causes for the Civil War.[10] Hawthorne's Revolutionary Tales, particularly "The Gray Champion" and "My Kinsman, Major Molineux," are, conversely, stories of a middle-class reaction to oppression by the few. To read Simms and Hawthorne as history is to see that by 1839 New England and the South had apparently fought two different Revolutionary Wars, both of them American.

One is inclined to forget that *The Scarlet Letter* is a frontier novel, even though Roger Chillingworth is recently ransomed from the Indians. Glimpses of frontier life are rare in the novel and are most noticeable in the opening scaffold scene and in the spectators who come to Salem for the Election Day ceremonies. But the forest, Hawthorne's symbol of the wilderness—the home of the "Black Man," the playground of the elf-child Pearl, and the place of assignation for Hester and Dimmesdale—broods over the novel. The actual frontier of the novel is Hawthorne's metaphor for the frontier of the human heart—the middle point between the freedom of the forest and the restraints of community morality.[11]

As Stanley T. Williams, F. O. Matthiessen, and others have pointed out, Hawthorne's obsession with individual sin and the ultimate cleansing power of the community is a legacy of Puritan thought and is indicative of what might be called the New England "mind." Williams gives an excellent summary of Hawthorne as a New England writer:

We can understand New England without Hawthorne; yet Hawthorne without New England we cannot comprehend. She was literally of his

10. C. Hugh Holman, "William Gilmore Simms' Picture of the Revolution as a Civil War," in Holman, *The Roots of Southern Writing: Essays on the Literature of the American South* (Athens, Ga., 1972), 35–49.

11. For a more detailed discussion of the presence of the frontier in *The Scarlet Letter,* see Edwin Fussell, *Frontier: American Literature and the American West* (Princeton, 1965), 91–114.

blood and brain; her scenes and her people form the stuff of his romances, and his own forefathers revisit the upper shades in his pages. . . .

Yes, it was the breath of his nostrils, this study of an invisible world, of whose existence he was in his way as firmly convinced as were Emerson and Thoreau. . . . That curiosity concerning the two fundamental relationships, of Man to God and Man to Man, which motivated the literature of New England, he shared, though his conclusions were neutral, inconclusive, even pessimistic.[12]

Hawthorne's New England is a moral as well as a physical location. As Simms's novels amplify the political concerns of his South, so Hawthorne's romances are set within the intellectual sphere of New England. It is not surprising that Hawthorne's frontier differs greatly in more than time, location, and climate from Simms's; they are portraits of two distinct regional cultures.[13]

Hawthorne's complaint in his preface to *The Marble Faun* about America's lack of "antiquity," "mystery," and "picturesque and gloomy wrong" seems to show him as having changed his position in the ten years since his "Custom-House" sketch, which introduced *The Scarlet Letter* (1850). In "The Custom-House," Hawthorne's narrator can find an old symbol in the attic of the Salem custom-house and, via "the moonlight of imagination," weave a powerful romance from it. A decade later, he complains of a lack of materials. His deprecation, however, is not that of a maturing author who discounts his juvenilia of a decade ago; rather, it is the statement of a writer who is attempting to abjure the regional in favor of the international. What Hawthorne may have discovered from the economic failure of *The Marble Faun* was that what was regionally powerful was not internationally translatable. Rather than a romance of Europe as he intended, Hawthorne's novel remains a romance of Americans in Europe and, like the Italians of "Rappaccini's Daughter," Hawthorne's Americans are fundamentally the characters of his New England romances who play out their parts against an exotic background. The weakness of *The Marble Faun* can perhaps be credited to Hawthorne's failure to adjust the moral

12. Stanley T. Williams, "Nathaniel Hawthorne," in *Literary History of the United States,* ed. Robert E. Spiller *et al.* (3 vols.; New York, 1974), I, 419.

13. In *The Development of American Romance: The Sacrifice of Relation* (Chicago, 1980), Michael Davitt Bell argues that the romance, as practiced in the latter half of the nineteenth century, was particularly suited to the intellectual tradition of New England.

climate of the novel to its international setting. Henry James was later to recognize the extreme difficulty of such an adjustment and to use it as a major theme in *The American, Portrait of a Lady, The Ambassadors,* and *Daisy Miller.*

Referring to a chapter of Simms's *Views and Reviews in American Literature, History, and Fiction* (1846), Simms's Young America manifesto, Hawthorne asserts: "We cannot help feeling that the real treasures of his subject have escaped the author's notice. The themes suggested by him, viewed as he views them, would produce nothing but historical novels, cast in the same worn out mould that has been in use these thirty years, and which it is time to break up and fling away." [14] Such a statement helps to illuminate the differences in the romance as Simms practiced it and as Hawthorne also did in *The Scarlet Letter* and less successfully in *The Marble Faun.*

Simms's advocacy of fidelity to an actual historical event and to the depiction of manners and customs was at odds with Hawthorne's view of the romance, which is centered on the exploration of an invisible moral world and is less bound to historical actualities. Yet in *The Scarlet Letter* and *The House of the Seven Gables,* Hawthorne's use of New England history and legend is what validates and makes possible his examination of the Puritan mind. Without the historical underpinnings—or to use T. S. Eliot's term, the "objective correlative"—which such locating provides him, Hawthorne's examinations would lose much of their power and even their credibility, as *The Marble Faun* exemplifies.

Simms's and Hawthorne's practice of the romance is consistent with the mind of their regions. Hawthorne's famous "Custom-House" definition of the romance as "a neutral territory, somewhere between the real world and fairy-land, where the Actual and the Imaginary may meet," is a definition in Puritan thought of the real frontier as the place where the "invisible world" may shape the community—a place where the actualities of the world are at the service of mind, belief, or faith. It is an idea found in Emerson's "transparent eyeball" and later in the poetry

14. William Gilmore Simms, "The Epochs and Events of American History, as Suited to the Purposes of Art in Fiction," in *Views and Reviews in American Literature, History, and Fiction,* ed. C. Hugh Holman (Cambridge, Mass., 1962), 30–127. The quotation from Hawthorne is cited in Randall Stewart, "Hawthorne's Contributions to *The Salem Advertiser,*" *American Literature,* V (1934), 331.

of Robert Frost—"The land was ours before we were the land's." [15] The dwellers in Hawthorne's Salem in *The Scarlet Letter* live on this intellectual frontier between the forest—the realm of superstition—and England—the epitome of godless civilization. The historical romance of Scott and its subsequent variations in Cooper and Simms finally have little in common with Hawthorne's depiction of a region whose controlling ideas and metaphors are ahistorical. From Jonathan Edwards' moral laws to Emerson's moral sense, Puritan thought and its subsequent manifestations in the New England mind were concerned finally with absolutes more than with circumstances. To reiterate Williams, "We can understand New England without Hawthorne; yet Hawthorne without New England we cannot comprehend." The regional context is as important to Hawthorne as it is to the reader.

This belief in the absolute has underlying it a necessary devaluation of the importance of the historical moment, except as that moment occasions moral confrontation. Hawthorne's romance is ultimately a story of interior rather than of exterior events, a form that finds its most extreme expression in Melville's *Moby-Dick*. What Hawthorne chooses for his romantic materials, the supernatural and the legendary, are often metaphorical expressions for a moral, or at least a psychological, state of mind. For this reason many modern readers have argued that Hawthorne is less a practitioner of the romance than a pioneer in psychological realism in fiction. This concern with the invisible world suggests clearly the reasons for Henry James's admiration of Hawthorne. One does not have to look hard to see Hawthorne and his New England heritage in James's novels. Isabel Archer and Lambert Strether are the direct descendants of Hester Prynne. They are all the inheritors of a New England tradition.

Simms's practice of the romance is closer in form to Cooper's and to Scott's than to Hawthorne's, but the ways in which Simms's historical romance differs from Scott's and Cooper's are indicative of the influence of his region on his work. They also suggest that the romantic tendencies of southern literature have their roots in a view of history that is augmented by but not born of the defeat of the Confederacy in the Civil War.

---

15. Robert Frost, "The Gift Outright," in *The Poetry of Robert Frost* (New York, 1970), 424–25.

Simms delineates these differences in his essay "The Writings of James Fenimore Cooper" in *Views and Reviews in American Literature, History, and Fiction.* He lauds Cooper for his championing of America as a subject for the historical romance, for "having struck the vein, and convinced the people not only that there was gold in the land, but that the gold of the land was good." Simms wrote: "To Mr. Cooper the merit is due, of having first awakened us to this self-reference,—to this consciousness of mental resources, of which our provincialism dealt, not only in constant doubts, but in constant denials." [16]

Yet Simms found much to criticize in Cooper, and in Scott as well. Simms had little patience with the Scottian formula of a hero caught and buffeted by historical forces beyond his control—a formula, as I have suggested, that Cooper inherited in his novels. Simms declared:

Mr. Cooper surrenders himself to the progress of events. He leaves to one to beget and occasion the other. Hence the desultory character of his writings; the violence of transition; the strange neglect to which certain of his characters are destined, in whom he at first strives to interest us; and the hard scramble, which the persons of the drama are compelled to make, each to get into his proper place, for the *tableau vivant,* at the falling of the curtain. . . . The whole machinery here is feeble, and a writer of romance cannot more greatly err than when he subjects his hero to the continual influence of events. We have no respect for heroes placed always in subordinate positions—sent hither and thither—baffled by every breath of circumstance—creatures without will, and constantly governed by the caprices of other persons. This was the enfeebling characteristic in Scott's heroes. [17]

In his preface to the 1853 edition of *The Yemassee,* Simms contends: "The modern Romance is the substitute which the people of the present day offer for the ancient epic. The form is changed; the matter is very much the same." [18] Inherent in Simms's contention is the difference between his use of the romance form and Scott's; he is not telling the story

16. Simms, *Views and Reviews,* 267, 266. For a full discussion of the relationship of Simms to Cooper, see Holman, "The Influence of Scott and Cooper on Simms," in *The Roots of Southern Writing,* 50–60.

17. Simms, *Views and Reviews,* 262.

18. William Gilmore Simms, *The Yemassee,* ed. Alexander Cowie (New York, 1962), 5.

of a historical period alone, but rather the history of a people and their society. Simms is often more social historian than romancer, and his characters influence rather than are influenced by the course of history. *The Yemassee,* the only Simms novel that is still read by students of American literature, is the story of one civilization overcoming another—the 1715 defeat of the Yemassee Indians by South Carolina settlers. Simms's concern with "civilization" and his often obsessive fidelity to historical fact separate his frontier romances from those of Cooper. In Simms's judgment, Cooper's romances lack (1) a diversity of characters to portray the society of the American frontier and (2) a complexity of plot and historical fact that coalesce to show the importance of the historical moment described. These faults, according to Simms, are what led Cooper to his complaint against his American materials:

Mr. Cooper entertained a notion, expressed in some one or more of his prefaces, that the literary material of his own country was too limited and too deficient in variety, to admit of frequent employment. He thought it too easily exhausted, and though he did not say so, it was very evident, at that time, that he thought he himself had already exhausted it. We need scarcely to say that we think all this a very great error. In Mr. Cooper's hands, no doubt, there would be a want of variety; not because of any deficiency in the material, but, simply, because the mind of Mr. Cooper is limited in its grasp. It is too individual in its aims and agencies,—does not often vary, but rather multiplies the same forms, characters, images and objects, through different media—now enlarging and now depressing them—now throwing them into greater shadow, and now bringing them out into stronger light—seldom entirely discarding them for others, and we should think not easily capable of doing so. His characters are uniformly the same, his incidents are seldom varied;—the whole change which he effects in his story, consists in new combinations of the same circumstances, heightened, now and then, by auxiliary events, which are seldom of much additional importance. In Indian life and sailor life, he was almost uniformly successful—for the simple reason, that such stories called simply for the display of individual character. They enabled him to devote his genius, as would be always the desire of his mind, to a single object. . . . To manage the progress of one leading personage, and to concentrate in his portraiture his whole powers, has been the invariable secret of Mr. Cooper's success. We very soon lose all interest in his subordinates.

Take away from his stories one or two of the personages, and the rest are the merest puppets.[19]

This concentration on the individual as emblematic of a society and its history is anathema to Simms's "epic" theory of the historical romance. In *Views and Reviews,* Simms carefully divides the historical romance into two literary provinces—that of the historian and that of the poet. Simms emphasizes the role of the historian, warning that fidelity to the historical moment is of ultimate importance because "if the ordinary citizen is at liberty to contravene your facts and dispute your premises, there is necessarily an end to your story." Given Simms's "epic" and, therefore, social intentions for the romance, such a response from the reader must be avoided. He continues:

> There must be a faith accorded to the poet equally with the historian, or his scheme fails of effect. The privileges of the romancer only begin where those of the historian cease. It is on neutral ground alone, that, differing from the usual terms of warfare, as carried on by other conquerors, his greatest successes are to be achieved.[20]

Like Hawthorne, Simms defines the romance as a "neutral" territory, but unlike Hawthorne's definition of it as the form "where the Actual and the Imaginary may *meet*" (italics mine), for Simms the Actual, or historical, and the Imaginary are at war, with history having the stronger hand. This is not history in the service of art so much as art in the service of social history.

In *The Yemassee,* Simms weaves together essentially three stories. The connecting story is the historical event—the 1715 uprising of the Yemassee Indians over a land dispute with South Carolina settlers and their subsequent defeat outside the Charleston settlement by a militia force led by Governor Charles Craven. The second story is the fall of Indian civilization, portrayed in the inflexibility of Sanutee, the Yemassee chief; in the corruption of his son, Occonestoga, by his contact with the white man; and in the heroism and love shown by Matiwan, Occonestoga's mother, who kills her son to prevent his dishonor before the tribe. The

19.   Simms, *Views and Reviews,* 273–74.
20.   *Ibid.,* 56.

third story is that of the white settlers—the love plot of Captain Gabriel Harrison (who is later discovered to be Governor Charles Craven in disguise) and a settlement girl, Bess Matthews. There are the rather stock capture, escape, pursuit, and rescue adventures of Harrison among the Indians and the defense of the settlement "Block-House" stockade by the whites. Though uneven and hackneyed in places, *The Yemassee* has a power that comes from Simms's ability constantly to weave together the line of each story into a fast-paced novel.

In *Views and Reviews,* Simms declares that "the usual and grand defect in all Mr. Cooper's stories" is that "in truth, there is very little story":

He seems to exercise none of his genius in the invention of his fable. There is none of that careful grouping of means to ends, and all, to the one end of dénouëment, which so remarkably distinguished the genius of Scott, and made all the parts of his story fit as compactly as the work of the joiner,—but he seems to hurry forward in the delineation of scene after scene, as if wholly indifferent to the catastrophe. The consequence is, that his catastrophe is usually forced and unsatisfactory. He is, for this reason, compelled frequently, at the close, to begin the work of invention;—to bring out some latent matter,—to make unlooked for discoveries, and prove his hero, be he hunter or pirate, to have been the son of somebody of unexpected importance;—a discovery which, it is fancied, will secure him [the hero] a greater degree of the reader's favour, than he could have before commanded.[21]

Simms's novel is the careful work of "a joiner." Each story line has its own integrity, and each is fitted together well, with the possible exception of the final defeat of the Yemassees outside Charleston, an episode that serves more as a historical afterword than as part of the novel proper. Simms's use of history is more than a backdrop for the story; as he himself mentions in his preface, many of the events of the story lines, though transposed, are well documented in historical accounts of the uprising.[22]

Simms's insistence on the role of history in the romance and on the function of the romance as modern epic suggests a use of the form that is different from the purposes of Hawthorne and Cooper. In proclaiming

21. *Ibid.,* 26–61.
22. See the account from the Boston *News-Letter* reprinted in Simms, *The Yemassee,* ed. Cowie, xlii–xliv.

The Yemassee "an *American* romance," Simms was insisting on his story as an epic—the story of a nation and its people. "It is the artist only who is the true historian," he declared, adding, "It is by such artists, indeed, that nations live." The epic impulse, according to Robert Kellogg and Robert Scholes, "is not a historical one, nor a creative one; it is re-creative."[23] The epic is written within an implied tradition and links society to that tradition; in other words, it is a narrative form with a social and public purpose that goes beyond the actual telling of the story itself. Simms's linking of the epic and the romance announces his political intention in the use of the romance form. His South Carolina settlers are seen as the inheritors of a tradition and culture that stretch back to Homer and Virgil, and that tradition is recast and retold to coincide with the values of his South of 1835. Hence, for Simms the social values of the novel are justified not only by the specific historical event described but also by Western tradition, and not only for a region but also for a nation and a race.

Vernon Parrington writes of Simms:

> If there had only been a little more of the intellectual in him, if he could have detached himself as an artist from the immediate and present, he might have risen superior to his unfortunate environment. . . . He must be partisan to a people and a cause, rather than to his art. The South that he loved was romantic, and he would appeal to the world as a South-erner. . . . He never realized what a clutter of useless luggage he carried into his study. It is a pity that he constricted himself to the shell of an outworn order, instead of realizing that social orders and institutions are significant to the novelist only as he stands apart from them, observing their ways and considering their interplay in the lives of men and women. It was a major loss to American letters that he should not have striven to be an artist first, and a southern romantic only at a later and more con-venient season.[24]

Perhaps Parrington is right that, had Simms striven to be more a national and less a regional writer—in other words, to be like Cooper—both the quality and the value of his work to American literature, as Parrington

23. Simms, *The Yemassee*, ed. Cowie, 6; Simms, *Views and Reviews*, 36; Robert Scholes and Robert Kellogg, *The Nature of Narrative* (New York, 1966), 12.
24. Parrington, *The Romantic Revolution*, 126–27.

defines it, would be much greater. But Parrington ignores the vital issue of Simms's work—that Simms's America *is* the South—and in doing so fails to understand that the strength of the work he admires, like Hawthorne's, is the result of a response to a regional culture. Simms could hardly ignore his "unfortunate environment"; it was not only the focus of his art, but the prime mover behind it as well. Simms's theory and practice of the romance are the direct result of the "immediate and present" needs of his region. He could hardly have appealed to the world as anyone else but a southerner.

The fire-eating secessionist Simms of the 1850s was a much different man from the Simms of the 1830s who opposed South Carolina's Nullification Doctrine and was for a time quite unpopular in Charleston for his vocal support of Andrew Jackson's policies. Yet to see Simms as a proponent of Jacksonian democracy is misleading. Simms loved the United States, and he loved the South; he never questioned the correctness of the nullification ordinance so much as the wisdom of it. As late as 1842, Simms described himself in a letter as being "an ultra-American, a born Southron, and a resolute loco-foco."[25] Like many southerners, including John C. Calhoun, Nathaniel Beverley Tucker, and George Fitzhugh, Simms believed in the right of individual states to determine their own laws, and like many southerners he subscribed to the idea of a Greek democracy in which all citizens, but not all men, were accorded equality. As suspect as this particular notion of democracy may seem, the tendency to align the South with Greek or Roman culture is clearly present not only in Simms's equation of the romance with the epic, but also throughout much of southern literature, finding its strongest modern restatements in the essays and poetry of Allen Tate.[26] Simms's avowed purpose in *The Yemassee* is to present a modern epic, and at its core the novel is about the most pressing issue of the South in Simms's day—racial supremacy.

Perplexing to some readers is Simms's compassionate and thorough

---

25. William Gilmore Simms, *The Letters of William Gilmore Simms,* ed. Mary C. Simms Oliphant, Alfred Taylor Odell, and T. C. Duncan Eaves (5 vols.; Columbia, S.C., 1952–1956), I, 319.

26. Allen Tate's *Essays of Four Decades* is perhaps the most important series of American essays examining the influence of Western tradition in American letters. Section IV is of particular interest to the concept of regional letters. See also Tate's *Collected Poems, 1919–1976,* esp. "Retroduction to American History," "The Mediterranean," "Aeneas at Washington," and "Aeneas at New York."

treatment of the Yemassee Indians. Unlike Cooper's Indians, who are invariably archetypes, "good" or "bad," Simms's Yemassee tribe possesses a complex cross-section of human flaws and virtues. The Indians have their virtual counterparts in the white settlement, and Matiwan, in the sacrifice of her son, achieves a level of noble pathos and courage unequaled by any other character in the novel. Throughout *The Yemassee* the fall of the Indians is treated as a genuinely tragic event, with all attendant pathos; but as Simms makes clear, it is an inevitable and necessary tragedy.

The first chapter of *The Yemassee* succinctly characterizes the height and the inevitable collapse of the Yemassee dynasty.

> In 1715, the Yemassees were in all their glory. They were politic and brave—a generous and gallant race. The whites had been welcomed at their first coming to their woods, and hospitably entertained; and gradually lost all their apprehensions, from the gentleness and forbearance of the red men. . . . Until this period the Yemassees had never been troubled by that worst tyranny of all, the consciousness of their inferiority to a power of which they, at length, grew jealous. . . . Their chiefs began to show signs of discontent, if not of disaffection, and the great mass of their people assumed a sullenness of habit and demeanour, which had never marked their conduct before. . . . Another and a stronger ground for jealous dislike arose necessarily in their minds with the gradual approach of that consciousness of their inferiority which, while the colony was dependent and weak, they had not so readily perceived. But, when they saw with what facility the new comers could convert even the elements, not less than themselves, into slaves and agents, under the guidance of the strong will and the overseeing judgment, the gloom of their habit swelled into ferocity, and their minds were busied with those subtle schemes and stratagems with which, in his nakedness, the savage usually seeks to neutralize the superiority of European armour. . . .
>
> A turn in the river unfolds to our sight a cottage, standing by itself, half finished, and probably deserted by its capricious owner. Opposite, on the other bank of the river, an Indian dries his bearskin in the sun, while his infant, wrapped in another, and lashed down upon a board,—for security, not for symmetry—hangs rocking from the tree.[27]

The white settlers of Simms's novel are not only inherently superior; they

27. Simms, *The Yemassee*, ed. Cowie, 11–13.

are actually so. Not only do they prove to be intellectually above the Indians, but they are better woodsmen and fighters as well. Simms's Indians are not Cooper's supermen. In the second chapter of *The Yemassee*, Sanutee, the chief of the tribe and its most renowned warrior, is bested at deer hunting by the piratical Chorley, and then again by Chorley in hand-to-hand combat. The noblest Indian is no match for the most scoundrelly of the whites, and the Indians' failure to put themselves under Harrison's protection leads them to be duped by Chorley into opposing the whites. As the fallen Occonestoga attests, the Indians are sadly but inevitably corrupted by the presence of a superior race.

The tragedy of the Yemassees' downfall and the inherent nobility they show in spite of their corruption are necessary to the epic quality that Simms wants to achieve in the story. The Indians are worthy foes. Their inevitable doom does not mitigate their tragic elevation, but rather validates their downfall. They die bravely, and their defeat elevates their conquerors.[28] If the Indian cannot survive the superiority of the white race in freedom, he dies with honor and a resignation to necessity. He loses his world without forsaking it or cheapening it, as exemplified in Sanutee's dying speech to Matiwan:

> It is good, Matiwan. The well-beloved has no people. The Yemassee has bones in the thick woods, and there are no young braves to sing the song of his glory. The *Coosah-moray-te* [Governor Craven] is on the bosom of the Yemassee, with the foot of the great bear of Apalachia. He makes his bed in the old home of Pocota-ligo [the Yemassee village], like a fox that burrows in the hill-side. We may not drive him away. It is good for Sanutee to die with his people. Let the song of his dying be sung.[29]

The nobility of the Indian, who was virtually extinct as a cultural force in the South of 1835, does not show up in the blacks of *The Yemassee*. In their opposition to the whites, the Indians are savage but admirable; at the end of the story the black slaves, momentarily released from the constraints of the whites, are brutally savage. After the whites defeat the Indians, the slaves begin a brutal wholesale slaughter of the survivors:

28. In *Anatomy of Criticism: Four Essays* (Princeton, 1957), 319, Northrop Frye notes: "It is hardly possible to overestimate the importance for Western literature of the *Iliad*'s demonstration that the fall of an enemy, no less than of a friend or leader, is tragic and not comic."

29. Simms, *The Yemassee*, ed. Cowie, 405–406.

But the pursuers were at hand, in the negroes, now scouring the field of battle with their huge clubs and hatchets, knocking upon the head all of the Indians who yet exhibited any signs of life. As wild almost as the savages, they luxuriated in a pursuit to them so very novel—they hurried over the forests with a step as fleet, and a ferocity as dreadful—sparing none, whether they fought or pleaded, and frequently inflicting the most unnecessary blows, even upon the dying and the dead.[30]

The final, telling portraiture of the baseness of Simms's Negroes is their attack on the dying Sanutee and their attempt to slaughter Matiwan, who is at Sanutee's side, a picture of fidelity. It is the noble victor, Governor Craven, who saves Matiwan and carries her "tenderly" away with all the respect due her nation.

Published just four years after Nat Turner's slave rebellion, *The Yemassee*'s final scene bears all the fears of the South toward the prospect of the free black man. Like the red man, the black cannot exist in freedom with the whites, but unlike the Indian, Simms's black has no real heroic stature. Hector, Gabriel Harrison's servant, does give his master a warning that saves the white man's life, but in this, his best quality, loyalty, Hector is equated with Harrison's dog, Dugdale, a fierce animal who is Hector's charge throughout the novel. In refusing the freedom that a grateful Harrison extends to him, Hector mouths Simms's litany on the place of the Negro in society:

"I d—n to h—ll, maussa, ef l guine to be free!" roared the adhesive black, in a tone of unrestrainable determination. "I can't loss you company, and who de debble Dugdale guine let feed him like Hector? 'Tis onpossible, maussa, and dere's no use for talk 'bout it. De ting aint right; and enty I know wha' kind of ting freedom is wid black man? Ha! you make Hector free, he turn wuss nor poor buckrah—he tief out of de shop—he git drunk and lie in de ditch—den, if sick come, he roll, he toss in de wet grass of de stable. You come in de morning, Hector dead—and, who know—he take no physic, he no hab parson—who know, I say, maussa, but de debble fine 'em 'fore anybody else? No, maussa—you and Dugdale berry good company for Hector. I tank God he so good—I no want any better."[31]

30.	*Ibid.*, 406.
31.	*Ibid.*, 392.

Hector "knows his place"; it is only his close association with the superior white man that keeps his savagery at bay. Without a master Hector, like Dugdale, would be lost. His servitude is charitable to his character.

Just as Hawthorne's explorations of the hidden world of the psyche reflect the mind of his region, so Simms's concern with social history and tradition reflects the heritage of his South. Implicit in his theory of the romance is the belief that the experiences of the past are the lessons and legacy of the present. For Simms, and for the public mind of his region in 1835, that lesson was of the historical, traditional, and social necessity of white supremacy for the South and for America.

In the frontier novels of Cooper, Hawthorne, and Simms we can see three different manifestations of the historical romance that constitute three different responses to the American settlement story—one national and two regional. Cooper, much more than Simms or Hawthorne, was committed to the idea of a single American experience, an experience that took place over distance rather than over time. Perhaps no other American writer was so convinced of or so powerfully conveyed the myth of the American as the new man in the new world as Cooper does in his Leatherstocking Tales. No other American author of Cooper's ability, perhaps with the exception of Thoreau, has so celebrated the individual character of the American. And certainly no other character in American fiction so perfectly embodies the romantic Promethean archetype as Natty Bumppo. He is the first man of America, a man exquisitely lacking a past, born wholly new on a land that renews itself westward.[32] Natty Bumppo is not a New Yorker, a New Englander, a southerner, or even a westerner; he is firmly an American—the member of no regional society. Leatherstocking's saga, which takes place approximately between the years 1740 and 1804, could be moved fifty years or more forward or backward in time, depending on the location of the novel, with only a few changes in the historical backdrop. Cooper's complaint against his American historical materials for the romance is finally a bit ironic; probably no major practitioner of the historical romance has felt less bound to his specific context than Cooper was in his conception of Natty Bumppo's story.

32. Cooper's archetypal successor becomes the western "cowboy" hero—the stranger with no known background or past who rides in from the sunrise and rides out, westward, with the sunset.

Simms and Cooper are aligned on opposite sides of the Scottian formula of the fusion of history and art. With Simms, art is at the service
of history; with Cooper, history serves art. Simms's concern is with the
history and character of a society. Cooper's imagination, and his subject,
are finally not historical at all; his concern is mythic, and larger than
Simms's—the idea behind the history and character of a nation.

Commenting on the mythic quality of the Leatherstocking saga, D. H.
Lawrence wrote:

> True myth concerns itself centrally with the onward adventure of the
> integral soul. And this, for America, is Deerslayer. A man who turns his
> back on white society. A man who keeps his moral integrity hard and
> intact. . . . This is the very intrinsic-most American. He is at the core of
> all the other flux and fluff.[33]

As Lawrence points out, Cooper's saga is not of America and its people
but of The American, the mythic progenitor of The Land of the Free.
Leatherstocking is bound by no region and by no social culture except
his "whiteness." Even in his death scene in *The Prairie,* Leatherstocking
has abjured the society of Ishmael Bush's entourage to die among the
Indians, who see him not as a representative of white society but as the
representation of The White—The Pathfinder, The Deerslayer. Bush and
the other "true" whites of the saga encompass only a small degree of the
idea of which Leatherstocking is the complete embodiment. Cooper set
out to write a national story and found that the national story he wanted
to tell was not of a people but of an archetypal individual.

In their regional romances Hawthorne and Simms are self-avowed
American writers. But their Americas are different places, with different
societies and differing values. *The Scarlet Letter* and *The Yemassee* are fictional histories of New England and the South, respectively. They are
not the stories of their protagonists so much as of the relationship of
those protagonists to their societies. As I have suggested, the form these
romances take, and even their authors' definitions of the form, are prod-
ucts of regional cultures. Given a history and a set of communal values,
Hawthorne and Simms create in their fiction a completed past that explains and measures the world of their present. This relationship between

---

33. D. H. Lawrence, *Studies in Classic American Literature* (New York, 1923), 92.

history and culture in the formulation of a past that informs the present
is what I call the historical imagination.

The terms *history* and *the past,* as I am using them, are similar but not
identical. History is the record of events, the fact; the past is the influence
of those events on the present. In other words, the past is history interpreted and made meaningful. In this way the past is connected with and
dependent upon the present, and, perhaps, on the expectation of the
future. To use Van Wyck Brooks's terms, the past is usable and believed,
often in spite of history. The historical imagination is concerned with
the past; it is the sense of the accumulation and influence of history in
the present.[34]

For Simms and for Hawthorne, the romance provided the perfect
literary mode for the expression of the historical imagination. Their
regions provided them with centuries of romantic historical materials
(which their nation did not), and the "minds" of their separate regions
provided them with valuations of that history. The differences in form
that the romance took for each writer are a result of the different attitudes
toward history that are implicit in the pasts of their respective regions.

As I have suggested, Hawthorne's view of history is, paradoxically,
ahistorical. History is a moral continuum in which the absolute is manifest in the particular; the hidden moral world is of greater importance
than the historical event that brings the invisible world into focus. The
neutral territory where the Actual and the Imaginary meet is not only a
definition of the creative process of romance, but also a definition of the
way in which the past is created—history interpreted—by the historical
imagination. It is a view of history that is particular to, though not necessarily the exclusive property of, the New England mind.

For Simms, history is a process rather than a continuum, which validates the present moment via the past. History and social history are
synonymous; history is the record of the continuing of civilization and
tradition into the present. The romance provides a twofold public purpose. It records the history of a people and their tradition, and it interprets
that history and applies it to the present. The past is the measurement of
and the clarifier of the present moment.

---

34. For a more theoretical account of the historical imagination, see R. G. Collingwood, "The
Historical Imagination," in *The Idea of History* (1946; rpr. New York, 1974), 231–49. See also Harry
B. Henderson, *Versions of the Past: The Historical Imagination in American Fiction* (New York, 1974).

That the romance survived and survives today in so much of southern fiction has many causes. Sociologically, the nineteenth-century South was not affected by the "melting pot" of immigration in anything like the way that the Northeast, the Midwest, and the Far West were, and the South has thus remained a more indigenous region than most of the country. Industrialization has spread in the South at a much slower pace than in the rest of the nation, and rural populations still predominate in many of the southern states. But the most important force behind the South's retention of its regional identity and its particular historical imagination lies in the fact that as the great national (and romantic) story of the American settlement became a national completed past, the South as region experienced another story, and in a different way from the rest of the country—the Civil War. As C. Vann Woodward has eloquently explained and explored in *The Burden of Southern History,* the southerner has inherited a past, and a historical consciousness of that past, that separates him from the rest of the country.[35]

In the controversies leading to the Civil War, in the war itself, and in the subsequent experience of Reconstruction, southerners were created in their regional mind, and in the national mind, as a separate people. Well over a century of technological advances, social change, and national crises have done little to erase the idea of the southerner as different from the rest of Americans. As a result the southerner of today, like the southerner of 1865, has a past alive in the present. And, importantly, that past is epic—the story of a people distinguished by their history from other American people. The southern writer is conscious of the past, of the epic myths of his region, of the necessity of confronting the past even in the technological present. The Civil War did not create the historical imagination of the South, but it continues to prolong it in the present, when it has diminished in the rest of the country.

As I have suggested, the romance form results in part from the historical imagination—the constant confrontation of the past in the present—and although the romance as a separate form of fiction has all but vanished in American letters, it is to this particular and inescapable and constant cognizance of the past that the prevalence of romantic elements in southern letters may in large measure be attributed.

35. C. Vann Woodward, *The Burden of Southern History* (Baton Rouge, 1960).

3

O Brave New World! The Rise of Midwestern Realism

The dominant mode of midwestern writing, from the Middle Border of the mid–nineteenth century to the Heartland of the twentieth, is realistic.

The term *realism*—like *romanticism, naturalism,* or *modernism*—is a Hydra to the literary critic who wishes to define his categories closely. Like the mythical monster who grows two heads for every one that is cut off, the term *realism* sprouts problems, contradictions, exceptions, influences, relationships, and theories in direct ratio to the more finely honed the definition applied to it is. To discuss realism as critical theory, as Howells, James, and the numerous critics who have succeeded them in this quest have done, is often to discuss the influence of Balzac, Flaubert, Turgenev, and Taine on a generation of well-informed and well-read authors. It is to differentiate between Balzac, Zola, and Huysmans; to separate schools, often not readily apparent, into Realistic, Prenaturalistic, and the Twilight writers. Or it is to weave a critical blanket large enough to cover Mark Twain and Henry James.

But to discuss realism as it applies to midwestern fiction is less to discuss the Continental literary theories than those tendencies in a literature that arise from the cultural ideas and assumptions of a region. Edward Eggleston and Edgar Watson Howe had not read extensively in the Continental realists when they composed *The Hoosier School-Master* and *The Story of a Country Town*. Yet they and other writers—Hamlin Garland, Caroline Kirkland, and Joseph Kirkland—were in general accord as to the form that literature should take. This was not because they were theoretical critics, although Garland's 1894 *Crumbling Idols* might give him some claim to this title, but because their experience of the Midwest and their desire to write about that region found expression through realistic techniques.

The reasons for this are twofold. First, realism is descriptive. The Midwest, as opposed to New England, the South, and the Middle States, was for many readers of the nineteenth century a "new" place; it compelled a description of its "exotics" almost as much as Virginia and North Carolina did from William Byrd almost a century and a half earlier. For this reason, Middle Border literature often contains travelogue tendencies—the assumption that the people, events, and customs are of interest to the reader in and of themselves, especially for a predominantly eastern readership. The verb tense here is important. The antebellum southern writer is often psychologically using the past tense—describing how Dixie *was* or comparing today with yesterday. Yet even though the actual tense of almost all fiction is the past tense, the psychological tense in which most of these early midwestern writers wrote is the present—things are the way they *are* described, not *were*. These are not historical novels; they are contemporary ones. In many ways they share the same psychological verb tense as William Byrd's and Captain John Smith's discovery narratives.

As description, realism treats things that are—actualities. Especially as practiced by midwestern writers, realism might be said to be the democratic mode of fiction because of its concern with the depiction of middle- and lower-class characters and its attention to the "unremarkable" day-to-day details of those characters' lives. Underlying this approach is the assumption that those events, characters, and objects merit such description. Whether a way of dress, a social custom, or a local dialect, whatever is described in fiction is to some degree, by virtue of that description, elevated. The description of a flower on a dunghill elevates not only the flower but the dunghill as well.

Realism—the "democratic" mode—is appropriate for the region the midwestern writer depicts because the history of the Midwest and its inhabitants is inextricably entangled with populist idealism. At its simplest it is the belief in the American republic as the government of and by the common man.[1] Implicit in the idea of the Midwest is the belief that it is a region that holds the promise of Jacksonian democracy, as opposed to the social and financial aristocracies of the South, the industrial North-east, and New England. This ideal accounts, in part, for the rise in the Midwest of the labor movement, free silver advocacy, the Grange, and other populist causes. At the same time, the ideal also accounts for a nationalistic fervor that could oppose such movements as "un-American." The Midwest is a region of political contraries under the same shared idea. It sent its young men to fight slavery in the South in the Civil War and also, as state militiamen and National Guardsmen, to fight the labor movements in Chicago and other cities. It is the region that could back Lincoln and Bryan and yet oppose Altgeld's social policies.

This discrepancy between the ideal and the actual, between theory and practice, is often at the heart of midwestern social realism. The result is a literature that at once glorifies the common man as the promise of America and yet depicts him as venal and narrow-minded and deplores it. Like his southern counterpart, the midwestern novelist is caught in an almost schizophrenic conflict between the ideal and the actual; but unlike the southerner, the midwestern writer can disclaim the past and rage against the present, in the hope, perhaps, of reclaiming and shaping the future. In the castigation of the present resides an idealism about the possibilities of the future. Much of midwestern realism offers a Gatsby-like hope for and belief in "the orgiastic future that year by year recedes

---

1. For a detailed discussion of populism and literature, see Smith, *Virgin Land*. For a historical study of midwestern populism in the late nineteenth and the twentieth centuries, see Russel B. Nye, *Midwestern Progressive Politics: A Historical Study of Its Origins and Development, 1870–1950* (East Lansing, 1951).

before us," a belief that, somehow, "tomorrow we will run faster, stretch out our arms farther." [2]

This dual tendency is clearly present as early as 1839 in Caroline Kirkland's *A New Home—Who'll Follow?* Written under the pseudonym of Mrs. Mary Clavers, Kirkland's account of her seven-year residence in backwoods Michigan takes the form of a long letter presumably written for the amusement of a society lady friend in New York. Though interlaced with romantic episodes and sketches, Kirkland's book is for the most part a detailed account of frontier life in Michigan in the middle 1830s. In her preface she admits to "glosses, and colourings, and lights, if not shadows, for which the author is alone accountable," but also maintains, "I felt somewhat tempted to set forth my little book as being entirely, what it is very nearly—a veritable history; an unimpeachable transcript of reality; a rough picture, in detached parts, but pentagraphed from the life." Eight years later, as literary editor of the *United States Magazine and Democratic Review,* Kirkland had become a firm advocate of realism in fiction: "Nine-tenths of the magazine stories, so popular among us, have nothing to do with this life," she asserted, "and fiction which has no relation to what has been, or what is to be, must be both vapid and valueless." [3] *A New Home—Who'll Follow?* suggests that her conversion to realism was, in large part, the result of her experiences on the Michigan frontier.

Fittingly for the story of a New York socialite's initiation into frontier life, Kirkland opens her book with an epigram from William Cullen Bryant. In one sense *A New Home* is the tale of the deromanticizing of the West for this eastern adventurer, who sets out on her "Rozinante" to find the frontier of "Hoffman's tour or Captain Hall's 'graphic' delineations." Through the course of the experiences she describes, her romantic notions of the West and the formal New York social proprieties she so dearly cherishes fall victim to the daily pragmatisms of frontier life. The narrator discovers that on the Middle Border one is dependent on one's neighbors, no matter how crude those neighbors might be by eastern standards. Like her pretensions, Kirkland's prized and "indispen-

2. F. Scott Fitzgerald, *The Great Gatsby* (New York, 1925), 182.
3. Caroline Matilda Kirkland, preface to *A New Home—Who'll Follow? or, Glimpses of Western Life,* ed. Sandra A. Zagarell (New Brunswick, N.J., 1990), 1; Kirkland, "Periodical Reading," *United States Magazine and Democratic Review,* XVI (January, 1845), 61.

sable" possessions are transformed to utilitarian purposes or thrown away; her china soup tureen becomes a chamber pot, her mahogany bureau finds employment as a corncrib, and her paper slippers completely disintegrate in a Michigan mudhole. After a full recital of the trials of log-cabin life—"skillet baths," snakes, and hard, tedious work—the narrator amusedly reflects that, before coming west, she had "dwelt with delight on Chateaubriand's *Atala,* where no such vulgar inconvenience is once hinted at; and my floating visions of a home in the woods were full of important omissions, and always in a Floridian clime, where fruits serve for *vivers.*" [4]

Kirkland learns to love the West, though more for what it can be than for what it is:

> After allowing due weight to the many disadvantages and trials of a new-country life, it would scarce be fair to pass without notice the compensating power of a feeling, inherent as I believe, in our universal nature, which rejoices in that freedom from the restraints of pride and ceremony which is found only in a new country. To borrow from a brilliant writer of our own, "I think we have an instinct, dulled by civilization, which is like the caged eaglet's, or the antelope's that is reared in the Arab's tent; an instinct of nature that scorns boundary and chain. . . ." This "instinct," so beautifully noticed by Willis, is what I would point to as the compensating power of the wilderness. Those who are "to the manor born" feel this most sensibly, and pity with all their simple hearts the walled-up denizens of the city. And the transplanted ones—those who have been used to no forests but "forests of chimneys," though "the parted bosom clings to wonted home," soon learn to think nature no step-mother, and to discover many redeeming points even in the half-wild state at first so uncongenial.[5]

This love is given with full attention to the realities of the harsh life of the West, a life, as Kirkland reiterates throughout *A New Home,* that is very different from the romantic descriptions of Chateaubriand, Cooper, Captain Hall, and Irving. Kirkland's praise of Michigan is also a manifesto on the necessity of realism to describe what is, at the core, the experience of the West. In her depiction of life on the Middle Border

4. C. M. Kirkland, *A New Home,* ed. Zagarell, 49.
5. *Ibid.,* 148.

she is calling for a new form of writing as well, in much the same way that Mark Twain will in *Life on the Mississippi*. Mark Twain's cub pilot goes from the romance of riverboating to the stronger and more vibrant actuality of running the Mississippi. It is not a daydreaming boy but an experienced pilot, and a literary realist, who writes:

> Now when I had mastered the language of this water and had come to know every trifling feature that bordered the great river as familiarly as I knew the letters of the alphabet, I had made a valuable acquisition. But I had lost something, too. I had lost something which could never be restored to me while I lived. All the grace, the beauty, the poetry had gone out of the majestic river! . . .
>
> No, the romance and the beauty were all gone from the river. All the value any feature of it had for me now was the amount of usefulness it could furnish toward compassing the safe piloting of a steamboat. Since those days, I have pitied doctors from my heart. What does the lovely flush in a beauty's cheek mean to a doctor but a "break" that ripples above some deadly disease? Are not all her visible charms sown thick with what are to him the signs and symbols of hidden decay? Does he ever see her beauty at all, or doesn't he simply view her professionally, and comment upon her unwholesome condition all to himself? And doesn't he sometimes wonder whether he has gained most or lost most by learning his trade?[6]

In her subsequent two-volume *Forest Life* (1842), Kirkland has more praise for the West, this time in direct contrast with the East:

> The contrast can be imagined only by those who have tried both. . . . [T]he difference may be compared to that which marks the course of the Niagara;—in one place rapids and cataracts agitating the mighty flood till the air is filled with a brilliant spray, and earth trembles to the deep-voiced roar of the waters; and again, after only a single bend in the river, a glassy, waveless expanse, whose onward movement is scarcely perceptible. Over the one may now and then be discerned a glorious rainbow, but the other reflects always the green and peaceful shores, and the bright and steady lamps of heaven. Yet I suppose one must be like the fish, cold-blooded, to prefer the still water.[7]

6. Samuel L. Clemens, *Life on the Mississippi* (1874; rpr. New York, 1968), 65–67.
7. Caroline Matilda Kirkland, *Forest Life* (2 vols.; New York, 1842), II, 230–31.

But such epiphanic moments are rare. In *A New Home,* Kirkland often has more invective than praise for the dwellers of her "Niagara." Like Howe, Garland, Lewis, Anderson, and others of the midwestern writers who would follow, Kirkland sees in the Midwest the potential for a ful-fillment of the democratic ideal, and having glimpsed the potential, she is all the more critical of the actuality she encounters. Though certainly no early populist—for to ignore Kirkland's patrician sympathies would be to distort her work greatly and to weaken its tension—she envisions a republic of first-rate men and women. Yet with only a few notable exceptions, *A New Home* is a gallery of sketches of second-, third-, and even lower-rate individuals who, taken together, constitute a mob-ocracy of ignorance and venality—a Jacksonian nightmare.[8]

Modern readers may find more amusement and less vexation than Kirkland does in her accounts of the unwillingness of her local Michi-ganders to take positions as servants "with an acknowledgement of in-ferior station," but they may sympathize with Kirkland's assertion:

> If the best man now living should honour my humble roof with his pres-ence—if he should happen to have an unfortunate *penchant* for eating out of the dishes, picking his teeth with his fork, or using the fire-place for a pocket handkerchief, I would prefer he should take his dinner *solus* or with those who did as he did.[9]

But although dress, table manners, social forms, and habits are amusing topics for Kirkland's eastern audience, the author of *A New Home* sees these things as manifestations of a greater problem—namely, the em-ployment of the democratic ideal of "equality" as justification for igno-rance and parochialism. Her concern is common to much of midwestern literature: the future of the American dream is in danger from a perver-sion of the very ideals that dream embodies.

> The better classes of English settlers seem to have left their own country with high-wrought notions of the unbounded freedom to be enjoyed in this; and it is with feelings of angry surprise that they learn after a short

---

8. For an examination of the perversion of republican ideals in Kirkland's characters, see John C. McCloskey, "Jacksonian Democracy in Mrs. Kirkland's *A New Home—Who'll Follow?*," *Michigan History,* XLV (December, 1961), 347–52.

9. C. M. Kirkland, *A New Home,* ed. Zagarell, 53.

residence here, that this very universal freedom abridges their own liberty to do as they please in their individual capacity; that the absolute democracy which prevails in country places, imposes as heavy restraints upon one's free-will in some particulars, as do the over-bearing pride and haughty distinctions of the old world in others; and after one has changed one's whole plan of life, and crossed the wide ocean to find a Utopia, the waking to reality is attended with feelings of no slight bitterness.[10]

Here again is the juxtaposition of the ideal and the reality, as exemplified on the Middle Border. After reading *A New Home,* one is perhaps justified in wondering if Kirkland is not speaking of her own experience as well as that of the English settlers in the region. If "eastern" is substituted for "English"—"the better classes of eastern settlers"—"cosmopolitan society" is substituted for "old world," and "the Alleghenies" is substituted for "the wide ocean," we have in summary the story of the experience of Kirkland's narrator.

Throughout her narrative Kirkland exposes what she deems to be the tyranny of the "Republican spirit," which manifests itself in both small and large ways as a perversion of the high ideals to which it lays claim. The ideal of a community of free men has degenerated into a practice of enforced "borrowing," which obligates Kirkland's narrator to lend anything and everything to any neighbor who demands it—staples, horses, razors, linens, china, garden plots. A request is even made for the narrator to lend her baby, a request she refuses. Even the loftiest sentiments of the American ideal are cheapened by the hard usage of the frontier republican. Perhaps the strongest example of this is found in Kirkland's sketch of the politician, Mr. Jenkins, "a muscular Rob-Roy" whose claims to integrity reside in his ability to intimidate any would-be detractor:

[Mr. Jenkins] had made up his mind to serve his country, and he was all this time convincing his fellow-citizens of the disinterested purity of his sentiments.

"Patriotism," he would say, "patriotism is the thing! any man that's too proud to serve his country aint fit to live. Some thinks so much o' them-

10.   *Ibid.,* 139–40.

selves, that if they can have jist what they think they 're fit for, they wont take nothing; but for my part, *I* call myself an American citizen; and any office that 's in the gift o' the people will suit *me*. I'm up to any thing. And as there aint no other man about here,—no suitable man, I mean— that's got a horse, why I'd be willing to be constable, if the people's a mind to, though it would be a dead loss to me in my business, to be sure; but I could do any thing for my country. Hurra for patriotism! them 's my sentiments.[11]

Court proceedings, town meetings, and elections are most often used to private advantage: "No matter at what distance these important affairs are transacted, so fair an excuse for a *ploy* can never pass unimproved; and the virtuous indignation which is called forth by any attempt at dissuading one of the sovereigns from exercising 'the noblest privilege of a freeman,' to forward your business and his own, is most amusingly provoking." Throughout *A New Home* Kirkland's narrator bridles at this rule of ignorance, and though she may be able to laugh at her own elitism, her amusement at the reverse snobbery of her Michigan neighbors is forced. She warns her eastern reader who may be setting out to find the American ideal in the Middle Border:

> He will find that he has no humble neighbours. He will very soon dis-
> cover, that in his new sphere, no act of kindness, no offer of aid, will be
> considered as any thing short of insult, if the least suspicion of *condescension*
> peep out. Equality, perfect and practical, is the *sine qua non;* and any ap-
> pearance of a desire to avoid this rather trying fraternization, is invariably
> met by a fierce and indignant resistance. The spirit in which was conceived
> the motto of the French revolution, "La fraternité ou la mort," exists in
> full force among us, though modified as to results.

Throughout her book, however, Kirkland makes it clear that the East is not necessarily preferable to the West. Occasionally she will soften state- ments like those above with remarks such as "all this forms part of the schooling which I propose for my spoiled child of refined civilization."[12] Though she often poses a bit as a cultural missionary among heathens, Kirkland's narrator also comes to consider herself a Michigander. And it

11. *Ibid.,* 171.
12. *Ibid.,* 48, 183–84, 185.

is this adoption of the frontier as her home that leads to her indignation. Though Caroline Kirkland did return to New York from the frontier, she did so after the publication of *A New Home.* The book was not written from a distance.

In particular for *A New Home—Who'll Follow?,* Caroline Kirkland deserves her place in midwestern and national letters. She was not only a pioneer of the Middle Border, but also a pioneer of what would become the dominant mode of fiction in the first half of the twentieth century. It is often difficult, in reading *A New Home,* to remember that Kirkland was a contemporary of Cooper, Simms, Irving, Emerson, and Hawthorne. Her book was published only four years after *The Yemassee,* three years after Emerson's *Nature,* two years after Hawthorne's *Twice-Told Tales,* in the same year as Longfellow's *Hyperion,* and it preceded *The Pathfinder, The Deerslayer,* and *The Scarlet Letter.* It is even arguable whether Kirkland was a fiction writer, though parts of *A New Home* are undisputably fictional; but there can be little argument about Kirkland's status as a realist. One need only compare her frontier with Washington Irving's romantic West in *A Tour on the Prairies* to see the difference in her attitude toward the subject. "I have never seen a cougar," Kirkland confesses on the first page of her book, "—nor been bitten by a rattlesnake." [13] Such sensational events are better left to other kinds of tales; Kirkland found the West in its actuality fresh enough to enrapture the imagination.

A comparison of Kirkland's *A New Home—Who'll Follow?* with the southerner John Pendleton Kennedy's *Swallow Barn; or, A Sojourn in the Old Dominion* (1832) can illustrate how differences in regional perspective affect narrative form. At first glance the scheme of the two works seems remarkably similar. [14] Kennedy's Mark Littleton is, like Kirkland's narrator, a New Yorker, and is visiting a Virginia plantation and writing his adventures in a long epistle to a friend in New York. In their prefaces both Kirkland and Kennedy disclaim any novelistic ambitions. In the structuring of their works they evidence certain debts to previous narratives,

---

13. *Ibid.,* 3.

14. William S. Osborne, ed., in his introduction to *Swallow Barn; or, A Sojourn in the Old Dominion,* by John Pendleton Kennedy (Philadelphia, 1832; rpr. of 1853 ed., New York, 1962), xxxviii, points out: "In some respects *Swallow Barn* anticipated Mrs. Caroline M. Kirkland's *A New Home—Who'll Follow?* (1839) with its sprightly style, its anecdotal air and its command of narrative without the excitement of high adventure."

and in particular to works of Washington Irving: *A Tour on the Prairies* and *Bracebridge Hall,* respectively.[15] And most significantly, both writers lay great emphasis on the accuracy and truthfulness of their accounts.[16]

In his preface to the 1832 edition of *Swallow Barn,* Kennedy admits that "I have had great difficulty to prevent myself from writing a novel," but maintains that "the country and the people are at least truly described." In his preface to the 1853 edition, entitled "A Word in Advance, from the Author to the Reader," Kennedy asserts that "Swallow Barn exhibits a picture of country life in Virginia, as it existed in the first quarter of the present century." He continues:

> Presenting, as I make bold to say, a faithful picture of the people, the modes of life, and the scenery of a region full of attraction, and exhibiting the lights and shades of its society with the truthfulness of a painter who has studied his subject on the spot, [these sketches] may reasonably claim their accuracy of delineation to be set off as an extenuation for any want of skill or defect of finish which a fair criticism may charge against the artist.[17]

Yet there is little in *Swallow Barn* to justify Kennedy's claim for realism. Although Kennedy must have hoped, through his use of a "Yankee" narrator, to achieve a semblance of objective reporting, as well as to assure the warm reception of an eastern audience, the world of *Swallow Barn* differs very little from the plantation life to be portrayed so romantically and nostalgically by Thomas Nelson Page in his postbellum fiction. Kennedy's Virginia is populated with honest rustics, knightly gentlemen, courtly ladies, and affectionate, as well as comic, slaves. The book is predominantly episodic and is tied together loosely by a comic plot involving a dispute between two plantations, Swallow Barn and the Brakes, over a worthless piece of land. Like the feuds of great families in romantic fiction, the dispute is brought to an end by the marriage of offspring of each plantation. Unlike Kirkland's use of humor, Kennedy's is not instructive, but is directed at endearing rather than exposing the Virginians.

15. In his introduction to *Swallow Barn,* Osborne gives a detailed discussion of Kennedy's debts to and reaction against the work of Irving.
16. Both Osborne and Jay B. Hubbell in *The South in American Literature, 1607–1900* (Durham, 1954), 481–95, accept Kennedy's portrayal of life in Virginia as basically realistic.
17. Kennedy, *Swallow Barn,* vii, 8, 10.

The politeness of the feud, a fistfight that vanquishes the village bully (entitled "A Joust at Utterance"), and a heroic hunt for a lady's lost hawk ("Knight Errantry") all serve gently and humorously to erect rather than to demolish an air of courtliness and chivalry at Kennedy's Virginia plantation.

Despite the discussions of farming, economics, and politics that are interspersed throughout the novel, *Swallow Barn* is a romantic picture of the Old Dominion. Noticeably missing in Kennedy's "true portrait" are lower-class whites and small planters.[18] There is little ignorance among Kennedy's southerners, no real poverty, and no disease.

Of Kennedy's inclusions, the most romantic portrayal is of slavery. It is only in the final chapters of the book that Kennedy addresses this issue. In "The Quarters," Mark Littleton, Kennedy's northern narrator, is taken for a tour of the slave cabins. Littleton notes:

> The air of contentment and good humor and kind family attachment, which was apparent throughout this little community, and the familiar relations existing between them and the proprietor struck me very pleasantly. I came here a stranger, in great degree, to the negro character, knowing but little of the domestic history of these people, their duties, habits or temper, and somewhat disposed, indeed, from prepossessions, to look upon them as severely dealt with, and expecting to have my sympathies excited towards them as objects of commiseration. I have had, therefore, rather a special interest in observing them. The contrast between my preconceptions of their condition and the reality which I have witnessed, has brought me a most agreeable surprise. I will not say that, in a high state of cultivation and of such self-dependence as they might possibly attain in a separate national existence, they might not become a more respectable people; but I am quite sure they never could become a happier people than I find them here.

Meriwether, the proprietor of Swallow Barn, sees slavery as a necessary evil in the ultimate civilization of the black race; he deplores the separation of man and wife and advocates laws "to forbid the separation under

18. Alexander Cowie, in *The Rise of the American Novel* (New York, 1948), 258–70, and Jay B. Hubbell both remark on the absence of lower- and middle-class whites in *Swallow Barn*. Hubbell's confidence in the realism of Kennedy's portrayal of Virginia plantation life is not, however, shaken by the omission.

any contingency, except of crime." Meant by Kennedy to be representative of southern whites' attitudes toward blacks, Meriwether wants to
set up a system by which "the most deserving" slaves would gain their
own tracts of land to farm and, eventually, "gain civil and criminal judicial
authority" over the other Negroes. Meriwether's problem, however, is
that the Negroes of Swallow Barn—such as Old Jupiter, the childlike
patriarch of the Quarter—have no desire for any such elevation of re-
sponsibility. In this Littleton concurs: " 'I suspect,' said I, 'Jupiter considers
that his dignity is not to be enhanced by any enlargement of privilege,
as long as he is allowed to walk about in his military hat as King of the
Quarter.' " [19] Jupiter, in Kennedy's account, is every bit as romantic a
character as Hector, Gabriel Harrison's servant in Simms's *The Yemassee*,
who staunchly refuses his freedom when it is offered to him by his master.

Although Old Lucy, a slave woman who mourns the death of her
estranged and criminal son in much the same way Molly Beauchamp
does in Faulkner's story "Go Down, Moses," is depicted as a figure of
great pathos and dignity, Kennedy's ennobling of her character does not
call into question the institution of slavery. For the most part Kennedy's
Negro is a romantic stereotype:

At present, I have said, he is parasitical. He grows upward, only as the
vine to which nature has supplied the sturdy tree as a support. He is
extravagantly imitative. The older negroes here have—with some spice of
comic mixture in it—that formal, grave and ostentatious style of manners,
which belonged to the gentlemen of former days; they are profuse of bows
and compliments, and very aristocratic in their way. The younger ones
are equally to be remarked for aping the style of the present time, and
especially for such tags of dandyism in dress as come within their reach.
Their fondness for music and dancing is a predominant passion. I never
meet a negro man—unless he is quite old—that he is not whistling; and
the women sing from morning till night. And as to dancing, the hardest
day's work does not restrain their desire to indulge in such pastime. . . .
Their gayety of heart is constitutional and perennial, and when they are
together they are as voluble and noisy as so many blackbirds. In short, I
think them the most good-natured, careless, light-hearted, and happily-
constructed human beings I have ever seen. [20]

19. Kennedy, *Swallow Barn,* 452–53, 459, 460.
20. *Ibid.,* 454–55.

Kennedy's claim that his idyllic pastoral is a "true portrait" of southern life must be considered in the context of *Swallow Barn*'s first publication in 1832 and also of its reissue in 1853. Although the novel was published in the same year as South Carolina's Nullification Act, no tension exists between Kennedy's southerners and their Yankee guest. Though they may have some political differences, they find themselves generally in accord. It is Kennedy's implicit warning that this accord must be preserved by allowing the South to solve her own problems. When Meriwether addresses the northern narrator, Kennedy is actually addressing his northern audience:

> "One thing I desire you specially to note: the question of emancipation is exclusively our own, and every intermeddling with it from abroad will but mar its chance of success. . . . We think, and, indeed, we know, that we alone are able to deal properly with the subject; all others are misled by the feeling which the natural sentiment against slavery, in the abstract, excites. They act under imperfect knowledge and impulsive prejudices which are totally incompatible with wise action on any subject. We, on the contrary, have every motive to calm and prudent counsel. Our lives, fortunes, families—our commonwealth itself, are put at the hazard of this resolve."[21]

It must be noted as well that although Kennedy's novel was published a year after Nat Turner's slave rebellion, which caused widespread terror among southern whites and resulted in brutal reprisals against blacks, only rarely do the actual events of Kennedy's day intrude in the world of *Swallow Barn*. Though the events of the novel are set in 1829, they are almost as far removed from the political, social, and economic issues of the day as Simms's Indian uprising in *The Yemassee* is from events contemporary with that novel's publication in 1835.

The revisions of *Swallow Barn* for the 1853 edition are mainly stylistic.[22] Kennedy, like Simms, opposed the Nullification Doctrine, but he never contracted secessionist fever; he often resided in Philadelphia and was a staunch Unionist. Both Kennedy and Simms, however, shared the same

---

21. *Ibid.,* 457–58.
22. In fact, the revisions Kennedy made were so minor, often involving only spelling or usage, that the 1853 edition is the one generally accepted by Kennedy scholars.

feeling of urgency about the right of the South to determine its own political destiny. In a March, 1851, letter to Simms, Kennedy wrote:

> The mawkish sentimentality which has been so busy of late in inventing sympathy for the pretended oppression of the negroes, it strikes me may render a new edition of Swallow Barn which is rather a good natured, and I am sure a true picture of the amiable and happy relations they hold to southern society—opportune at this moment, and so far as it may be well received an antidote to the abolition mischief. [23]

Kennedy's message to Simms is clear; the past, the romantic past of *Swallow Barn,* is perhaps a tonic for the ills of the present. What was true in 1832 was true in 1853, and again on the novel's republication in 1860 as the country drew closer to the edge of national calamity, and again on the novel's reissue in 1865 following the defeat of the South and the beginning of Reconstruction.

Though clearly there are propagandistic views in *Swallow Barn,* it would be wrong to see Kennedy merely as a propagandist for the South— as wrong as it would be to view Kirkland as no more than an eastern snob reacting to the coarseness of the dwellers of the Middle Border frontier, even though evidences of such snobbishness may be found throughout *A New Home.* Rather, as regional writers, both may be taken at their word that, in intent at least, they have presented a "true picture" of the regions they depict.

For both writers the true region is not necessarily contemporary with them. For Kirkland the real Midwest is found in the promise of the future, which the present must live up to and become. For Kennedy the true South is the romantic South—the idealized and harmonious past that the present must strive to recapture. Whether either imagined region has ever existed as described is finally irrelevant; both have existed and continue to exist in the regional consciousness that shapes both the form of American fiction and American literature in general.

Caroline Kirkland's portrayal of the Midwest in *A New Home* was followed by several decades of conventional love stories played out against a Middle Border background. These stories, the best of which are exemplified by the novels of two sisters, Metta V. Victor and Frances Fuller

23. Cited by Osborne, ed., in his introduction to *Swallow Barn,* xl.

Barritt, are sentimental love plots in which genteel eastern protagonists serve as cultural ambassadors to the rude West.[24] As Henry Nash Smith has pointed out, at the heart of such novels is "the theory of social stages which places the West below the East in a sequence to which both belong. The West has no meaning in itself because the only value recognized by the theory of civilization is the refinement which is believed to increase steadily as one moves from primitive simplicity and coarseness toward the complexity and polish of urban life."[25] Certainly this social theory, as Smith articulates it, is present in Kirkland's work, as is the conventional and unconvincing love story that comprises most of the final chapters of *A New Home*. Implicit in Kirkland's work and missing in these other novels, however, is a sense of the Midwest as possessing its own intrinsic values and possibilities (however unrealized they may be) that are independent of the East.

It was, in part, a reaction to this social theory that led Edward Eggleston to compose *The Hoosier School-Master* (1871).[26] Eggleston's novel marks the beginning of a school of late-nineteenth-century midwestern writers, including Edgar Watson Howe, Joseph Kirkland, and Hamlin Garland, who were committed to the idea of the Midwest as a subject for fiction and committed to realism as a literary method. In his preface to the 1871 edition of *The Hoosier School-Master*, Eggleston remarks:

> It used to be a matter of no little jealousy with us, I remember, that the manners, customs, thoughts, and feelings of New England country people filled so large a place in books, while our life, not less interesting, not less romantic, and certainly not less filled with humorous and grotesque material, had no place in literature. It was as though we were shut out of good society.[27]

It is difficult to view *The Hoosier School-Master* as a great novel, or as

24. Metta V. Victor, *Alice Wilde, the Raftsman's Daughter. A Forest Romance and The Backwoods Bride. A Romance of Squatter Life.* Both Beadle's Dime Novels. Frances Fuller Barritt, *East and West; or, The Beauty of Willard's Mill and The Land Claim. A Tale of the Upper Missouri.* Also Beadle's Dime Novels.

25. Smith, *Virgin Land,* 229.

26. Edward Eggleston, *The Hoosier School-Master,* Library Edition (New York, 1892). All references are to this edition, which was revised from the 1871 edition only in spelling and in an additional preface by the author.

27. Cited in Smith, *Virgin Land,* 235.

one that fully lives up to the intentions of its author. Its central character, schoolmaster Ralph Hartsook, grows out of the New England tradition that Eggleston argues against in his preface.[28] The mystery/love plot of the novel borders on the preposterous. Yet in spite of these basic flaws, Eggleston's novel contains ideas crucial to the development of midwestern literature and shows the first important attempt to use the Midwest as a subject for a sustained narrative.

In his 1871 preface Eggleston asserts that "our Western writers did not dare speak of the West otherwise than as the unreal world to which Cooper's lively imagination had given birth."[29] Whatever its demerits of central character and plot, *The Hoosier School-Master* attempts to describe the life particular to Eggleston's Indiana region—from climate to rural life to social customs, most notably the "spelling school." Most important in the novel is Eggleston's consistent attempt to reproduce Hoosier dialect. Acknowledging James Russell Lowell's *The Biglow Papers* as his model, Eggleston continues, "I may claim for this book the distinction, such as it is, of being the first of the dialect stories that depict a life quite beyond New England influence."[30] Although at least one critic has taken exception to the author's claim for accuracy in his depiction of Hoosier speech, Eggleston's use of dialect is not only a feature of the novel, but is of fundamental importance to it.[31] Implicit in Eggleston's claim, and throughout the novel itself, is the idea that dialect is not merely a different way of utterance, but rather the expression of such a difference. For example, when Eggleston's local hero, Bud Means, reinterprets Protestant liturgy into his creed of the church of "the best licks," he has not only vernacularized the religious principles but has also re-created them meaningfully for his region.[32]

Important also is Bud Means's status as a hero in the novel. He is farm-

28. Anthony Channell Hilfer, in *The Revolt from the Village, 1915–1930* (Chapel Hill, 1969), 36, contends that Hartsook is "a thoroughly conventional and genteel character whose manners and values in no way differ from those of any cultivated Easterner."

29. Cited in Smith, *Virgin Land*, 235.

30. Eggleston, *The Hoosier School-Master*, 7.

31. Anthony Hilfer argues that "Eggleston's interest in Hoosier dialect and manners is little more than mere antiquarianism" (*The Revolt from the Village*, 36).

32. Eggleston apparently took Bud Means's conversion seriously; in the 1880s he founded the Church of Christian Endeavor in Brooklyn and served for a brief period as its pastor. In his 1891 preface, he mentions that this church is the Church of the Best Licks rendered into "respectable English" (*The Hoosier School-Master*, 25).

bred and has none of the pretensions to refinement and ancestry so common in earlier midwestern love stories. This use of the regional character as hero, even though he is superseded in heroism by Ralph Hartsook, is important to Eggleston's establishment of a social theory opposed to the New England notion of class. Bud exemplifies a social theory of "character" as opposed to class, a theme that runs throughout midwestern fiction.

Like Simms and like Hamlin Garland, Eggleston was a strong proponent of regional literature. In his preface to the 1892 "Library Edition" of *The Hoosier School-Master,* he proclaims:

> The taking up of life in this regional way has made our literature really national by the only process possible. The Federal nation has at length manifested a consciousness of the continental diversity of its forms of life. The "great American novel," for which prophetic critics yearned so fondly twenty years ago, is appearing in sections.[33]

In such a statement, Eggleston is calling attention to his region's differences from the rest of the nation and from other regions as well. In doing so, he became one of the first midwestern writers to assert that the midwestern character was not merely an eastern character in an exotic setting, but rather was created by and possessed an indigenous mind and culture. Eggleston's claims to realism were based not only on his painstaking attention to dialect and his portrayal of local customs and life-styles, but also on his aversion to a social theory based on class. His labeling of his work as "provincial realism" was another way of affirming the integrity of the "provincial" as defined by eastern standards. For all the sentimentality of his story, Eggleston's Indiana is not a place of honest rustics in pure pastoral happiness. For every Bud there is a bully. Courts, political offices, and public institutions such as the poorhouse and the orphanage are susceptible to corruption by the dishonest and venal. The present of *The Hoosier School-Master* is not perfect or even nearly so; the American dream has not been realized in Flat Creek, Indiana. But for Eggleston, through the "character" of men like Bud Means it may yet be.[34]

---

33. *Ibid.,* 6–7.

34. It is interesting that both Caroline Kirkland and Edward Eggleston became vocal social reformers in New York after their experiences with rural life in the Midwest.

In E. W. Howe's *The Story of a Country Town* (1883) and Joseph Kirkland's *Zury: The Meanest Man in Spring County* (1887), the optimism for
the future so prevalent at the ending of *The Hoosier School-Master* has all
but vanished. Howe's novel offers the first real expression of the bleakness
and inherent desperation of small-town and farm life on the Middle
Border that were to be further developed by Hamlin Garland in *Main-
Travelled Roads,* continued by Sherwood Anderson in *Winesburg, Ohio,*
and expressed at their blackest by O. E. Rölvaag in *Giants in the Earth.*
Although the title of Howe's novel suggests otherwise, the first third of
The Story of a Country Town takes place in the farming district, and many
of the subsequent events of the novel also take place outside the town.
There is, however, no real town/country division in Howe's attitude
toward the region; Howe's town, Twin Mounds, is only an intensification
of his country settlement, Fairview.

Fairview is no romantic pastoral setting, as Howe's somewhat neurotic
narrator, Ned Westlock, makes clear in the opening chapter of the novel.
In Ned's first words are the romantic aspirations of the Middle Border
settlers: "Ours was the prairie district out West, where we had gone to
grow up with the country." The rest of the story is the comparison of
the reality of Middle Border life with all the expectations such a statement
would imply. By the end of the novel, that dream of the West has become
a nightmare. Although Ned admits that "everyone who came there
seemed favorably impressed with the steady fertility of the soil," he adds
that Fairview was not the fulfillment of the promise of the western ad-
venture, and concludes, "when anyone stopped in our neighborhood, he
was too poor and tired to follow the others." Aside from the fertile soil,
little else is inviting in Westlock's description of Fairview:

> On the highest and bleakest point in the county, where the winds were
> plenty in winter because they were not needed, and scarce in summer for
> an opposite reason, the meeting-house was built, in a corner of my father's
> field. This was called Fairview, and so the neighborhood was known.
> There was a graveyard around it, and cornfields next to that, but not a
> tree or shrub attempted its ornament, and as the building stood on the
> main road where the movers' wagons passed, I thought that, next to their
> ambition to get away from the country which had been left by those in
> Fairview, the movers were anxious to get away from Fairview church, and

avoid the possibility of being buried in its ugly shadow, for they always seemed to drive faster after passing it.[35]

At the conclusion of this chapter Westlock hints that the barrenness of Fairview has taken its psychological as well as physical toll on its residents, and in particular on himself. Reflecting on his childhood years in the farming settlement, he remarks: "When I think of the years I lived in Fairview, I imagine that the sun was never bright there (although I am certain that it was), and I cannot relieve my mind of the impression that the cold, changing shadow of the gray church has spread during my long absence and enveloped all the houses where the people lived."[36]

In Howe's description of rural life is the recurrent theme of a dusty road (a theme that was to serve Garland as metaphor in *Main-Travelled Roads*), of backbreaking labor on an unforgiving land, and of the almost bestial obstinacy of the farmer trying to wring a small subsistence out of his continual labor. Ned's description of Fairview makes the settlement appear to be a secular manifestation of the hell that his father, the Reverend John Westlock, constantly put before the eyes of his congregation. Ned's father's religion and the land are paralleled throughout the country episodes of the novel. Ned summarizes his settlement's feelings about religion by stating that it "was a misery to be endured on earth, that a reward might be enjoyed after death."[37] Fairview and Twin Mounds comprise the location of that miserable endurance.

If the Fairview district is hell, then Twin Mounds is its ninth circle. In his description of the town's citizens, Howe demolishes the idea of the small-town citizen as the strong backbone of the nation. Ned remarks:

> The only resident of Twin Mounds who ever distinguished himself ran away with a circus and never came back, for although he was never heard of it was generally believed that he must have become famous in some way to induce him to forego the pleasure of returning home in good clothes, and swaggering up and down the street to allow the people to shake his hand.[38]

35. E. W. Howe, *The Story of a Country Town,* ed. Claude M. Simpson (Cambridge, Mass., 1961), 7–9.
36. *Ibid.,* 15.
37. *Ibid.,* 16.
38. *Ibid.,* 143–44.

Through Ned's descriptions of the townspeople, Howe paints a damning portrait of the narrowness, maliciousness, and hypocrisy of Twin Mounds' citizens.

> I never formed a good opinion of a man there that I was not finally told something to his discredit by another citizen, causing me to regard him with great suspicion, and if I said a good word for any of them, it was proved beyond question immediately that he was a very unscrupulous, a very ridiculous, a very weak, and a very worthless man. . . .
>
> As I grew older, and began to notice more, I thought that every man in Twin Mounds had reason to feel humiliated that he had not accomplished more, but most of them were as conceited as though there was nothing left in the world worthy of their attention. Their small business affairs, their quarrels over the Bible, and an occasional term in the town council, or a mention for the legislature or a county office, satisfied them, and they were as content as men who really amounted to something.[39]

The plot of *The Story of a Country Town* provides a thorough debunking of romantic notions of the Heartland. Ned's father leaves the ministry to become the proprietor of a newspaper and then runs off with a married woman. "Discontent is my disease," he writes in an explanatory note to Ned. Ned's mother is slowly worn down by her husband's brooding, by the harshness of her life, and then by her husband's elopement and her solitude; she dies with "a look of inexpressible grief on her face." Through his cheerful nature and hard work, Jo Erring, Ned's young uncle and childhood friend, becomes a successful tradesman and marries his refined sweetheart, Mateel, after a storybook romance; but the region takes its toll on even so robust a figure as Erring. He becomes moody, then pathologically jealous of his wife; he rejects her, and, when she divorces him and becomes engaged again, he murders her fiancé. He ends by committing suicide in the Twin Mounds jail, and Mateel dies from shock and illness. All the bright dreams of adolescence are destroyed by the reality of the present. Even the populist revolt of the farmer comes under Howe's attack, in the character of Biggs, the organizer of the farmers' collective who runs his own farm ineptly and who passes off pathetic homilies as wisdom.

39. *Ibid.*, 195–97.

Ned does marry Agnes, the schoolmistress, and tells us at the end of the novel that he is "worth considerable money." And in the honest characters of the Meeks and Big Adam, too, there is a glimmer of hope in Howe's otherwise desperate picture of the midwestern small town; but that hope is dim. At the end of the novel Ned and Agnes, though they have an income that does not require them to work, still reside in Twin Mounds, trapped in its narrowness. The novel closes with the note on which it began—the tolling of the Fairview church bell, in requiem for the dead, over the desolate and unforgiving landscape.

Howe's sympathetic and realistic portrayal of the small town met with approval from other American realists. Mark Twain remarked in a letter to Howe, "Your picture of the arid village life is vivid, and what is more, true. I know, for I have seen and lived it all." William Dean Howells wrote to Howe, "I have lived in your Country Town, and I know it is every word true." [40] Hamlin Garland was to acknowledge Howe as influential in his own decision to become a writer.

Though others, like Joseph Kirkland, objected to what they saw as melodrama in Howe's novel, and though any modern reader will be struck by the chain of unlikely coincidences that leads to the improbable conclusion that Damon Barker is Agnes' long-lost father, *The Story of a Country Town* is an uneven but important early realistic American novel. It pointed to and influenced a trend in midwestern literature that would become increasingly prevalent in the twentieth century—the idea of the Midwest as the land of a promise lost.

Joseph Kirkland's *Zury: The Meanest Man in Spring County* (1887) contains as dark a picture of midwestern life as *The Story of a Country Town,* but this darkness is somewhat mitigated by Kirkland's use of humor and the tall tale, in much the same way that Mark Twain uses humor as a device in "The Man That Corrupted Hadleyburg." Kirkland, like his mother Caroline Kirkland, shatters the notion of romantic primitivism that has been so often associated with the settlement of the Midwest. Like Eggleston's *The Hoosier School-Master, Zury* is notable for Kirkland's fidelity in his depiction of the dialect of the region that he describes, and much of the tall-tale humor that runs throughout the novel is a result of this vernacular.

40. Cited by Claude M. Simpson, ed., in his introduction to *The Story of a Country Town,* by Howe, ix, xii.

But unlike Eggleston's Hoosiers, Kirkland's Zury Prouder is an ambivalent character. Zury's most interesting feature is his native slyness and intelligence, with which he elevates himself from a poor settler's son to be the richest and "meanest"—stingiest—man in Spring County, Illinois, and eventually to election to the legislature. At first Zury seems to have much more in common with the "Flush Times" humorist Johnson Jones Hooper's Simon Suggs, whose motto is "it is good to be shifty in a new country," than with Eggleston's good-hearted Bud Means. But unlike Hooper's scalawag, and like Bud Means, Zury's most redeeming quality is his honesty. As Kirkland's character shows, however, honesty is not necessarily paired with generosity or compassion. As one Spring County resident remarks of Zury:

> Gimme a man as sez right aout "look aout fer yerself," 'n' I kin git along with him. It's these h'yer sneakin' fellers th't's one thing afore yer face 'n' another behind yer back th't I can't abide. Take ye by th' beard with one hand 'n' smite ye under the fifth rib with t'other! He [Zury] pays his way 'n' dooz 's he 'grees every time. . . . He knows haow t' trade, 'n' ef yew don't, he don't want ye t' trade with him, that's all; ncr t' grumble if ye git holt o' the hot eend o' th' poker arter he 's give ye fair notice. Better be shaved with a sharp razor than a dull one.

Zury, whose name is short for "Usury," sees his honesty mainly in economic terms:

> Honest? Me? Wal, I guess so. Fustly, I would n't be noth'n' else, nohaow; seck'ndly, I kin 'fford t' be, seeing' 's haow it takes a full bag t' stand alone; thirdly, I can't 'fford t' be 'noth'n' else, coz honesty 's th' best policy.[41]

His dictum that "honesty pays" is crucial to an understanding of his character. The reader is often left to wonder what Zury's character might be like if honesty did not literally pay. Kirkland's farmer has no time to discourse eloquently on the virtues of country life or the feeling of freedom that comes from open spaces. Zury is a pragmatic farmer, a materialist; he works the land to make money. Money, he claims, is "suth'n'"

41. Joseph Kirkland, *Zury: The Meanest Man in Spring County,* introduction by John T. Flanagan (1887; rpr. Urbana, 1956), 86–87.

th't's got t' be dug outer the graoun' 'n' then traded off fer suth'n' th't's growed a-top o' graoun' . . . suth'n 'r other th't takes labor." [42]

Money is the motivation behind most of Zury's actions in the novel. He marries twice, to increase his wealth and because he needs another hard worker. What he learns from suffering under the mortgage system is to "have a holt of the right eend of the poker," and he vows that if he ever gets a mortgage on someone, "it 'll sizzle his hands, tew, afore I'll ever let up on him." As a poor farmer, he can declare, like Caroline Kirkland's Michiganders, "Borryin' 's a need-cessity 'n' payin' 's a luxury," but when he becomes wealthier, he becomes an advocate of swift repayment.[43] He even reclaims a puppy from a child who has defaulted on a payment. "Business is Business!" is his motto.

Kirkland's description of the Prouder family's settlement in Spring County is perhaps the best portrait of the realities of farm life in nineteenth-century midwestern fiction. The oppressiveness of the mortgage system, the death of Zury's sister from the cold of winter and the harshness of farm work, Mrs. Prouder's giving her wedding ring to the local doctor as payment for a bill—all serve as clues to Zury's character. Kirkland's detailed descriptions of clearing land, "niggering" logs, raising hogs, "girdling" trees, and other day-to-day processes of farm life serve to create a picture harshly different from the idealized notions of settler life found in many earlier novels about the Midwest.[44]

For all his "meanness," Zury emerges in the novel as a product of his region, a hero if only because of his ability to survive his early years with determination and a native good humor. He is the realist's Horatio Alger hero, who pulls himself up through "pluck," but with little reliance on "luck." He gets ahead because he means to do so, and he never forgets what he is about.

Zury is an uneven novel. Kirkland is at his best in the early chapters in which he describes the Prouder family's battle with the land and Zury's ultimate success as a farmer. The love plot between Zury and Anne Sparrow (later Anne McVey), a New England schoolmistress who has come to Spring County for adventure, has been called by Henry Nash

42. *Ibid.*, 349–50.
43. *Ibid.*, 53, 59.
44. See also John T. Flanagan, "Joseph Kirkland, Pioneer Realist," *American Literature,* XI (1939), 273–84.

Smith "one of the strangest matings in all literature."[45] In spite of Zury's unconvincing transformation into generosity of character and spirit brought about by Anne's influence upon him, the schoolmistress serves a necessary function in the novel. She is the outsider whose romantic notions are tempered by her experience in the West. Her education in the novel is much the same education about midwestern life that Kirkland wanted to bring to his reader.[46] Through Anne we see the romantic dream meet the reality of farming. The odor of the horse barn vanquishes the New Englander's idyllic notion of the "natural" life. Where Anne sees an acre of beautiful forest, Zury sees firewood and the backbreaking labor of clearing the ground for crops. Anne finds money of little importance until her own is destroyed in a fire and she must seek financial help from Zury.

But Anne is useful to Kirkland in other ways than merely as a contrast to Zury. As Anthony Hilfer has pointed out, Anne's point of view aids Kirkland in "polemicizing against the ugliness of the farm and the village." Kirkland's frequent switching of the novel's focus from Zury to Anne allows him to comment on aspects of midwestern life that would escape Zury's notice. For example, in a chapter that opens with Anne's awaking on her first morning in Spring County, Kirkland gives the following description:

All night the world is a lovely, half veiled Danaë; with break of day she becomes a squalid, unkempt, disorderly invalid. A blue, unwholesome-looking haze spreads over every flat space, and the rays of dawn silver its surface with a pale, sickly light. The day which is refreshing at night-fall is dank at daybreak. Ague, like the ghost of a giant snake, crawls visible over the land: men shudder at the sight, and their flesh creeps at its very hideousness.[47]

Through Anne's observations Kirkland makes clear that he is describing,

45. Smith, *Virgin Land,* 243.

46. Dorothy Anne Dondore, in *The Prairie and the Making of Middle America: Four Centuries of Description* (Cedar Rapids, Iowa, 1926), 326, has another opinion of Anne's character in the novel. She writes: "The fact that the majority of the men of Zury's type do not find an Anne McVey furnishes the key to the work of many of the later rebels." This view of Anne as Zury's savior is justified in terms of the ending of the novel, but it does not take into account that Kirkland, although obviously fond of his character, deprecates her romantic notions of the West.

47. Hilfer, *The Revolt from the Village,* 41; J. Kirkland, *Zury,* 106.

but not necessarily praising as Eggleston did, the rural life of the Midwest. Rather, he is drawing a realistic portrait, and Anne's observations of the squalor of the district and the intolerance and ignorance of its inhabitants provide him with an observer's eye necessary to his portraiture.

Ultimately Kirkland's portrait of rural life in the Midwest is as damning as Howe's. Zury's unlikely reformation, brought about by his marriage to Anne, offers no real solution for the future of the region. If Kirkland objected to what he saw as melodrama in Howe's novel, he must have been aware of the failure of Zury's sentimental ending. What promise there is for the future of Kirkland's region lies in the integrity of hard work, which Zury has learned. When Zury goes to the legislature, he is disillusioned by the inefficiency and lack of diligence he finds there; but instead of being able to effect change, he returns home determined not to seek reelection. It is not in social institutions but rather in the "character" of Zury, in his notion of hard work and in his ebullient good humor, that the possibility of a brighter future for his region resides, though it is a possibility rarely glimpsed in the novel.

In *Zury: The Meanest Man in Spring County,* Kirkland advances the cause of midwestern realism. He is the first Midwestern fiction writer to portray closely the day-to-day rigors of farm life. He takes up from and excels Eggleston in the use of native dialect and folklore. In his account of Zury's and Anne's night together on the river and her subsequent pregnancy (which is "legitimized" by her brief marriage to another man), Kirkland became the first major midwestern writer explicitly to explore sexual matters in his fiction, though he revised the "offending" sections for later editions of the novel.[48] But perhaps the most important of Kirkland's contributions to midwestern fiction was the inspiration he offered for Hamlin Garland, whom he called "the first actual farmer in American literature" and whose works he championed.[49]

In Garland's fiction, particularly in the stories that comprise *Main-Travelled Roads* (1891), the Middle Border of the nineteenth century finds

48. For a detailed examination of Kirkland's use of sex in *Zury* and his later revisions of those passages, see Benjamin Lease, "Realism and Joseph Kirkland's *Zury,*" *American Literature,* XXIII (1952), 464–66.

49. For an account of the Garland-Kirkland relationship, see Clyde E. Henson, "Joseph Kirkland's Influence on Hamlin Garland," *American Literature,* XXIII (1952), 459–63. For Garland's own account, see Hamlin Garland, *A Son of the Middle Border* (New York, 1917).

its most complete expression. Garland spent much of his childhood and adolescence on farms in Wisconsin, Iowa, and the Dakotas, living as a child the life he was later to describe in his fiction.[50] *Main-Travelled Roads* and *Crumbling Idols* (1894), Garland's literary manifesto, are the result of his dedication to realism, or "veritism," as a literary creed to describe the economic and social conditions of his region. Carl Van Doren remarks, "The romancers had studied the progress of the frontier in the lives of its victors; Garland studied it in the lives of its victims."[51] Taken as a whole, *Main-Travelled Roads* dealt the strongest blow yet to the nineteenth-century romanticization of rural life in the Midwest; but, paradoxically, it affirms an idealistic possibility for the region's future—a possibility that rests firmly on a belief in the midwestern dream of democracy.

In *A Son of the Middle Border* (1917), an autobiographical account of his childhood and early adulthood, Garland reflects:

> I saw no humor in the bent forms and graying hair of the men. I began to understand that my own mother had trod a similar slavish round with never a full day of leisure, with scarcely an hour of escape from the tugging hands of children, and the need of mending and washing clothes. I recalled her as she passed from the churn to the stove, from the stove to the bedchamber, and from the bedchamber back to the kitchen, day after day, year after year, rising at daylight or before, and going to her bed only after the evening dishes were washed and the stockings and clothing mended for the night.
>
> The essential tragedy and hopelessness of most human life under the conditions into which our society was swiftly hardening embittered me, called for expression, but even then I did not know that I had found my theme.[52]

Garland is describing here a revelation that came to him when he returned to South Dakota in 1887 for a visit with his parents after having been three years in Boston, where he had spent much of his time at-

---

50. The most complete description of Garland's childhood experience with farm life and its influence on his fiction is Donald Pizer's *Hamlin Garland's Early Work and Career* (Berkeley, 1960). For a critical/biographical overview of Garland's career, including his later "romantic" period, see Joseph B. McCullough, *Hamlin Garland* (Boston, 1978).
51. Carl Van Doren, *The American Novel, 1789–1939* (New York, 1940), 226.
52. Garland, *A Son of the Middle Border*, 366.

tending public lectures and reading voraciously in the public library. There he read Eggleston, Howe, and Kirkland for the first time, became acquainted with William Dean Howells, and was exposed to the poetry of Whitman, the philosophical treatises of Spencer, and the theories of Darwin and Taine. Perhaps of most importance, he read Henry George's *Progress and Poverty* and enlisted himself in George's Single Tax advocacy, a movement to eliminate the tenant farmer system that had become so prevalent an evil in the Midwest. By the time Garland made his visit to his family in South Dakota, he had already become an orator and organizer for farmers' groups, and was later to be a professional campaigner for the Farmers' Alliance and for the People's Party. It was from this background of political and theoretical thought that Garland was to see in South Dakota and the rest of the Midwest the material for the stories that were to become *Main-Travelled Roads*.

It is almost impossible to separate Garland's political populism from his literary credo of "veritism" as he expounds it in *Crumbling Idols*. Veritism is, in fact, literary populism; Garland himself asserts the political implications of his literary theory:

> If the past was the history of a few titled personalities riding high on obscure waves of nameless, suffering humanity, the future will be the day of high average personality, the abolition of all privilege, the peaceful walking together of brethren, equals before nature and before the law. And fiction will celebrate this life.

For Garland, romanticism is reactionary; it supports and verifies traditions and structures that are essentially aristocratic. Realism is progressive; by depicting life as it is, a need for change and the reason for that need are clearly shown. For all his Darwinian references in *Crumbling Idols,* Garland is a populist idealist who sees in the idea of democracy the possibility of a better future:

> The realist or veritist is really an optimist, a dreamer. He sees life in terms of what it might be, as well as in terms of what it is; but he writes of what is, and, at his best, suggests what is to be, by contrast. He aims to be perfectly truthful in his delineation of his relation to life, but there is a tone, a color, which comes unconsciously into his utterance, like the sobbing stir of muted violins beneath the frank, clear song of the clarionet;

and this tone is one of sorrow that the good time moves so slowly in its approach.[53]

Notwithstanding the idealistic "softness" of *Crumbling Idols,* Garland's "veritism," as practiced in *Main-Travelled Roads,* is perhaps the toughest and most unmitigatedly realistic description of the physical and psychological hardships of rural life to be found in midwestern fiction. Its mood is bitter, its tone angry, even in Garland's dedication of the volume to his parents, "whose half-century pilgrimage on the main-travelled road of life has brought them only toil and deprivation."[54]

The world presented in these stories is bleak. In "Among the Corn-Rows," the romantic courtship of the country swain and the blushing farmer's daughter is thoroughly debunked as Rob, allowing himself ten days away from his work to find a wife, leaves his homestead and returns to his old settlement, where he proposes to Julia, who accepts the proposal in order to escape the backbreaking labor in the cornfield she is forced by her father to do. Even after the engagement is made, Rob hesitates to kiss his betrothed. "I guess we c'n get along without that," she says. In "The Return of a Private" a Civil War veteran, wounded and almost unrecognizable to his wife, returns home from the war to the grim realities of the mortgage system and of poverty. In "Under the Lion's Paw," perhaps the best story in the collection and certainly the most famous, a homesteader who has lost his farm because of a locust blight rents a run-down farm from a land speculator with the intention of buying it at a later date. After he has built improvements on the farm and made it productive enough to begin buying it, the owner raises the price because of the value of the improvements the farmer has made. "But *you* had nothin' t' do about that. It's my work an' my money," the farmer protests. "You bet it was; but it's my land," the owner answers. "Don't take me for a thief," he continues. "It's the law."[55]

Two of the stories, "A Branch Road" and "Up the Coolly," concern men returning home to visit the farm country after long absences. Each is struck by how different the realities of farm life are from the romantic

53. Garland, *Crumbling Idols,* 39, 43–44.
54. Hamlin Garland, *Main-Travelled Roads,* introduction by William Dean Howells (1891; rpr. New York, 1899), iii.
55. *Ibid.,* 108, 142, 143.

memory he had formed at a distance. In "A Branch Road" the visitor finds his old sweetheart worn down by poverty and fatigue, and unloved and brutalized by her husband. He persuades her to give up her marriage and run away with him. In "Up the Coolly" a successful actor returns home to find that his family have lost their farm and are living in poverty as tenant farmers. At first he believes that his brother's anger and resentment toward him stem from his unwitting neglect of the family and from the contrast between his "gleaming white cuffs" and his brother's muck-covered overalls. Later the actor comes to realize that he is the cause of his brother's anger because, in neglecting the plight of his home people, he has become part of the oppressing class. "A man like me is helpless," his brother declares. "Just like a fly in a pan of molasses. There's no escape for him. The more he tears around the more liable he is to rip his legs off." Even when the actor attempts to buy back the family farm, his brother will not accept it—not because of pride, but because of his own weary sense of defeat: "I'm a dead failure. I've come to the conclusion that life's a failure for ninety-nine per cent of us. You can't help me now. It's too late." [56]

In this farmer's resignation is the ultimate tragedy that runs through *Main-Travelled Roads.* That tragedy is the defeat of the human spirit of Garland's characters as they wage their "daily running fight with nature and against the injustice of [their] fellow-men." Nature, the land, is not always a brutal or antagonistic force; there is a beauty, almost epiphanic, to be found in the land throughout these stories; but the residents of the Middle Border have become too numb from their hardships to see it or to draw consolation from it. Nor is the character of the people of these farms necessarily brutal or savage. Garland's farmers, as a group, are good people, willing to share their few joys with their friends and quick to give such aid and consolation as they can. It is rather the corrupt few, supported by corrupt laws and institutions, who have defeated these men and women. Given a fair economic chance, and by extension a chance for comfort and for education, these stories say, such "heroic" men and women, by force of muscle and spirit, can conquer the land. As the farmer in "Under the Lion's Paw" says before he learns that he is to be cheated, "We begin to feel's if we was gitt'n' a home f'r ourselves; but

56.   *Ibid.,* 76, 87.

we've worked hard. I tell you we begin to feel it . . . and we're goin' t' begin to ease up purty soon." [57]

In a review for *Harper's Magazine* that was reprinted as an introduction to *Main-Travelled Roads,* W. D. Howells comments: .

> The stories are full of those gaunt, grim, sordid, pathetic, ferocious figures, whom our satirists find so easy to caricature as Hayseeds, and whose blind groping for fairer conditions is so grotesque to the newspapers and so menacing to the politicians. They feel that something is wrong, and they know that the wrong is not theirs. The type caught in Mr. Garland's book is not pretty; it is ugly and often ridiculous; but it is heart-breaking in its rude despair.

Howells' uneasiness over the savage realism of his protégé is evident both in this passage and in a later one in which he briefly notes that the ending of "A Branch Road" is "morally wrong." [58] Howells and Joseph Kirkland, who in an 1893 essay in the *Dial* had advised realists, "Let only truth be told, and not all the truth," had not taken realism to the political and investigatory extremes that Garland did in his collection. [59] Garland's dictum for the veritist—"Write of those things of which you know most, and for which you care most. By so doing you will be true to yourself, true to your locality, and true to your time"—is in general accord with Howells' theory of realism as being "nothing more and nothing less than the truthful treatment of material." [60] But Howells' assertion that fiction writers "concern themselves with the more smiling aspects of life, which are the more American, and seek the universal in the individual rather than the social interests," found no echoing response in Garland's veritism. [61]

---

57. *Ibid.,* 129, 141.

58. William Dean Howells, introduction to *Main-Travelled Roads,* by Garland, 3, 4.

59. Cited by John T. Flanagan in his introduction to *Zury: The Meanest Man in Spring County,* by Kirkland, v. It is interesting that Kirkland's statement is accompanied by his revision of *Zury* to eliminate the passages concerning sexuality that had offended many readers. Garland was to have the same problem with his novel *Rose of Dutcher's Coolly* (1895). Being regarded as a scandalous book, however, made Harold Frederic's *The Damnation of Theron Ware* (1896) an immediate financial success.

60. Garland, *Crumbling Idols,* 30; William Dean Howells, *"Criticism and Fiction" and Other Essays,* ed. Clara Marburg Kirk and Rudolf Kirk (New York, 1959), 38.

61. Howells, *Criticism and Fiction,* 62. It is interesting to note that Howell's boyhood experience in the Midwest as a printer's son was vastly different from the hardship endured by Garland in his

Main-Travelled Roads is Garland's most highly regarded work. Though he wrote and published numerous novels and collections of fiction during his career, only this collection and *Rose of Dutcher's Coolly* continue to excite critical interest, the latter mainly for Garland's bold use of sexual themes. Later on, Garland retreated from realism to romantic stories of the West and, with what must be seen now as a commonplace paradox, became a marketable writer.[62] His motivation may have been the poor sales of *Main-Travelled Roads* and his other early fiction, or the brief furor surrounding *Rose of Dutcher's Coolly,* or perhaps, as Larzer Ziff has suggested, because Garland had become comfortable as a literary figure in Chicago, where he had resettled. Very likely all these reasons had something to do with the change. In any event, the onetime veritist ended his career firmly affiliated with the genteel tradition.

The anger so often present in *Main-Travelled Roads,* as well as Garland's concern with the present and his commitment to the idea of literary realism as a remedy for social ills, was transmitted to a new generation of writers who continued that tradition long after Garland had rejected it, literally for greener pastures. In the first quarter of the new century Floyd Dell, Sherwood Anderson, and Sinclair Lewis were to carry midwestern social realism to its fullest expression. In the work of these writers, however, one rarely glimpses the idealism that lies just below the surface in Garland's and Caroline Kirkland's work. Rather, the anger of these new social realists was born less from the fear that the democratic ideal was in danger than from a disillusioned belief that perhaps it was already dead. It will be in Willa Cather's novels that the midwestern ideal is again glimpsed, but for that expression, Cather would break out of the mold her predecessors had shaped.

---

childhood. This might in some way account for Howells' reluctance to support farmers' movements, though he was extremely active in other causes. When Garland turned the focus of his fiction away from the Midwest, as Howells had done for most of his career, Garland's realism became less politically assertive and more closely resembled that of Howells.

62. Larzer Ziff, *The American 1890s: Life and Times of a Lost Generation* (New York, 1966), 93–108. See Also Bernard I. Duffey, "Hamlin Garland's 'Decline' from Realism," *American Literature,* XV (1953), 69–74; and Charles T. Miller, "Hamlin Garland's Retreat from Realism," *Western American Literature,* I (1966), 119–29.

4

A History Reinterpreted, a Past Discovered: Ellen Glasgow and Willa Cather

The historical imagination, the sense of the accumulation and influence of history on the present, informs much of southern fiction. The predominant literary mode of expression for the historical imagination in the nineteenth century was the romance. Although William Gilmore Simms wrote several tales of his contemporary southern frontier (often referred to as his "border romances"), the most significant body of his fiction is constituted by *The Yemassee* (1835) and seven romances of the Revolutionary War in South Carolina: *The Partisan* (1835), *Mellichampe* (1836), *The Scout* (1841), *Katharine Walton* (1851), *Woodcraft* (1852), *The Forayers* (1855), and *Eutaw* (1856).[1] John Pendleton Kennedy,

---

1. The "border romances" include *Guy Rivers* (1834), *Richard Hurdis* (1838), and *Beauchampe*

the only other antebellum writer of fiction who rivals Simms in prominence, used the colonial South as the setting of two historical romances, *Horse-Shoe Robinson* (1835) and *Rob of the Bowl* (1838). Taken together, Simms's and Kennedy's historical romances depict a period that spanned some eighty years. After the defeat of the Confederacy, the colonial South and the American Revolution were superseded in historical prominence in southern fiction by the Civil War and the decade immediately preceding it. The richness of southern history as a subject for fiction was thereafter telescoped into a period of approximately fifteen years.

Nowhere is this telescoping so evident as in the work of the romancer John Esten Cooke. Cooke's antebellum romances, *Leather Stocking and Silk* (1854), *The Virginia Comedians* (1854), and *Henry St. John, Gentleman* (1859), are set in colonial Virginia. But following the Civil War, in which he served as a captain in the Army of Northern Virginia until the surrender at Appomattox, Cooke made a reputation and a considerable livelihood writing chivalric romances of the Confederacy: *Surry of Eagle's-Nest* (1866), *Mohun* (1869), and *Hilt to Hilt* (1869). Though a reader of today would readily agree with Louis D. Rubin, Jr., that "only the fiercest chauvinism can make *Surry of Eagle's Nest* . . . into palatable literature," a postwar audience, especially in the North, praised the novel as a masterpiece. In *A Certain Measure,* Ellen Glasgow recounts an anecdote in which a prominent widow of Richmond tells her, "I do not deny that there is truth in your book; but I feel that it is a mistake for Southern writers to stop writing about the War. . . . If only I had your gifts, I should devote them to proving to the world that the Confederacy was right. Of course, I know that even the best novelists are no longer so improving as they used to be; but I have always hoped that . . . you . . . would write another *Surry of Eagle's Nest.*" [2]

Well over five hundred Civil War novels had been written by 1957, and yet, after so prodigious an outpouring, there appears (even now) to

---

(1842). Only *Beauchampe,* Simms's romance of the Beauchampe-Sharpe "Kentucky Tragedy," receives much critical attention from modern scholars; and that attention, for the most part, is because the novel is a fictional account of a historical event that has fascinated other American writers, among them Edgar Allan Poe (*Politian*) and Robert Penn Warren (*World Enough and Time*). *The Scout* was originally titled *The Kinsmen; Woodcraft* first appeared as *The Sword and the Distaff.*

2. Louis D. Rubin, Jr., "The Image of an Army: The Civil War in Southern Fiction," in *Southern Writers: Appraisals in Our Time,* ed. R. C. Simonini, Jr. (Charlottesville, 1964), 51–2; Ellen Glasgow, *A Certain Measure: An Interpretation of Prose Fiction* (New York, 1943), 84.

be little to refute Rubin's assessment: "There is no *War and Peace* about the South and its army. There is not even *A Farewell to Arms*. All we have is *Gone with the Wind,* a novel comparable only in physical size." Perhaps the finest nineteenth-century fictional accounts of the conflict are to be found in Stephen Crane's *The Red Badge of Courage* (1895) and John William De Forest's *Miss Ravenel's Conversion from Secession to Loyalty* (1867), but neither of these is an account of the Confederacy. Cooke's novels, the fiction of Thomas Nelson Page, and a plethora of other southern romances and tales codified the myth of the plantation and the chivalric tradition of southern aristocracy, which had its literary beginnings in Kennedy's *Swallow Barn,* into what became generally recognized as the Southern Tradition—the nostalgic, moonlight-and-magnolia presentation of the Old South and the Lost Cause. The immense popularity of Page's apologetic elegies for a lost romantic culture in *In Ole Virginia* (1887) and *Red Rock* (1898) is testimony not only to the region's but also to the nation's identification of the South with the plantation myth. As C. Hugh Holman has commented, "In the period between 1890 and 1910, when the historical novel flourished everywhere, the South seemed to be winning in the book stalls the war it had lost on the battlefield."[3]

If the defeat of the Confederacy provided the stimulus for numerous romances, it also led to the stagnation of the southern literary imagination. The glorification of the Lost Culture, as the romance usually presented it, did not allow the historical imagination to bridge the gap between the past and the present, between what was lost and what remained. With the Civil War as the crucial event and the historical romance as the vehicle for communicating and interpreting that event, the southern romancer found himself left with a past that found no intersection in the present and allowed for none in the future. The southern romance was no longer using history to interpret and to make meaningful the present; rather, in the work of the moonlight-and-magnolia writers, past and present were separated by an ever widening gap. Rather than interactive, the romance had become escapist.

In the postbellum South the overriding public issues were social and

---

3. Rubin, "The Image of an Army," 53. In *Fiction Fights the Civil War: An Unfinished Chapter in the Literary History of the American People* (Chapel Hill, 1957), Robert A. Lively examines more than five hundred historical novels of the Civil War. C. Hugh Holman, *The Immoderate Past: The Southern Writer and History* (Athens, Ga., 1977), 42.

economic. Though slavery was no longer an active institution, the South's greatest social adjustment was to be made on the racial question—a question that became increasingly complex as many of the old patrician families found themselves descending the economic ladder while the former slaves and the "poor white" and middle classes were ascending.

George Washington Cable was one of the few southern writers who successfully made this social reorganization the theme of a historical novel. Cable's *The Grandissimes* (1880) is set in New Orleans in 1803, immediately after the Louisiana Purchase. The novel explores two basic themes: racial equality between Honoré Grandissime and his quadroon half brother, an F.M.C.—free man of color—who also bears the name Honoré; and the social reorganization of New Orleans Creole culture by the incorporation of Louisiana into the United States.[4] Louis D. Rubin, Jr., has labeled *The Grandissimes* "the first 'modern' Southern novel" because of its "uncompromising attempt to deal honestly with the complexity of Southern racial experience."[5] Equally important is Cable's attempt to present the dilemma brought to southern society by the disintegration of a culture based on social hierarchy and its eventual replacement with a culture based on an economic formulation. In fact, these two themes are worked out in a complex formula whereby economic necessity is the catalyst that brings together the two Honorés in the business firm "Grandissime Brothers."

The Grandissimes is a curious blend of historical romance and realistic novel of manners. Much of the power and flavor of the novel comes from Cable's close examination of Creole society in New Orleans. The romantic temperament of the Creoles themselves is balanced by Cable's use of irony in his descriptions.[6] His condemnation of the Creoles' treatment of blacks finds its strongest expression in his depictions of the torture of Bras-Coupé, the capture and death of Clemence, and the suicide of black

---

4. For the major positions on *The Grandissimes,* see Richard Chase, *The American Novel and Its Tradition* (Garden City, N.Y., 1957), 167–76; Cowie, *The Rise of the American Novel,* 557–62; and Jay Martin, *Harvests of Change: American Literature, 1865–1914* (Englewood Cliffs, N.J., 1967), 101–105. The *Southern Quarterly,* XVII (Summer, 1980), contains seven articles on *The Grandissimes* in celebration of the centennial of that novel's publication. See also Louis D. Rubin, Jr., *George W. Cable: The Life and Times of a Southern Heretic* (New York, 1969), and Arlin Turner, *George W. Cable: A Biography* (Durham, 1956).

5. Rubin, *George W. Cable,* 78.

6. For a discussion of Cable's use of irony in *The Grandissimes,* see William Bedford Clark, "Humor in Cable's *The Grandissimes,*" *Southern Quarterly,* XVIII (Summer, 1980), 51–59.

Honoré. Yet at the center of this novel are the romantic genealogy of the Grandissimes, which is traced back to an Indian princess, and the gothic legend of the voodoo curse of Bras-Coupé. The plot is the romantic tale of an ancient feud between two great families—the Grandissimes and the De Grapions—which is laid to rest at the end of the novel by the promise of a future marriage between white Honoré, the head of the Grandissime family, and Aurora Nancanou, a direct descendant of the De Grapions.

Cable's novel was situated in a time and place that allowed him to bridge the past and the present and to project that past into the problems he saw in postbellum southern society. The New Orleans of 1803 not only allowed him to examine the collapse of a social order, but also provided him with free black characters with which to explore his theme of racial injustice. Although slavery is a present evil in *The Grandissimes,* Cable's deepest examinations are of free blacks—Palmyre, Clemence, and black Honoré. As in Cable's New South of 1880, however, the specter of slavery broods over his New Orleans of 1803—especially in the legend of Bras-Coupé. In *The Grandissimes* and in some of the tales of *Old Creole Days* (1879), Cable found the situation that allowed him the fullest play of the power of historical imagination. In his later polemical novel, *John March, Southerner* (1894), Cable was to include many of the same social themes he explored in *The Grandissimes;* but without the historical dimension, the novel was much less successful.[7]

In the use of the romance form and the role of the historical imagination, there are many similarities between *The Grandissimes* and *The Yemassee,* but Cable and Simms use the form to different purposes—Simms to uphold a social order and Cable to call that order into question. These differing purposes are reflected in the different emphases of the novels' forms: Simms uses realistic techniques in order to validate his romance; Cable uses romantic elements of southern history in his realistic examination of social problems. In *The Grandissimes,* knights and cavaliers have become literally the stuff of the masquerade ball that opens the novel. By the end, the projected marriages of Honoré and Aurora and of Frowenfeld and Clotilde promise future happiness for a property manager and a pharmacist.

7. Much like Hamlin Garland, Cable later retreated almost entirely from realism and wrote nostalgic romances of the Old South. *The Cavalier* (1901) was his greatest financial success.

The Grandissimes fused the historical romance and the realistic novel of manners, and thus predicted the direction that southern letters would take in the twentieth century. In the romantic tale of the feud between two great families and in his use throughout the novel of gothic legend, Louisiana folklore, and the mysterious past, Cable is an adept practitioner of the romance. In his descriptions of New Orleans and of the manners of its society, his careful attention to Creole and black dialects, and his depiction of cultural upheaval, he is an accomplished realist. In particular, Cable's novel demonstrates that the historical imagination, the sense of the accumulation and influence of the past in the present, is not antithetical to the literary practice of realism.

This movement in southern literature from romance to realism was to find its fullest expression in the first quarter of the new century, in the Virginia novels of Ellen Glasgow. In all, Glasgow published nineteen novels between 1897 and 1941, but her reputation in American letters rests chiefly on her thirteen novels of Virginia and on her collection of prefaces, *A Certain Measure* (1943). In the preface to *The Battle-Ground,* Glasgow describes her "novels of the Commonwealth" as "a social history of Virginia from the decade before the Confederacy." [8] She divides these novels into three groups, the first group of six novels constituting a history of Virginia from 1850 to 1912, a second group of three "novels of the country" spanning the period from 1894 to 1933, and a third group containing four "novels of the city" covering the years from 1910 to 1939.

That Glasgow began her Virginia novels with such a plan in mind is dubious, but the interlocking elements of the thirteen books do lend much credibility to the assumption that quite early in her sequence Glasgow did conceive such a pattern. [9] Whatever the case, the Virginia novels do work as a set, as most critics have willingly conceded. I am interested,

---

8.   Glasgow, *A Certain Measure,* 3.

9.   Studies of Glasgow abound. See esp., *Ellen Glasgow: Centennial Essays,* ed. M. Thomas Inge (Charlottesville, 1976); Blair Rouse, *Ellen Glasgow* (New York, 1962); Alfred Kazin, *On Native Grounds: An Interpretation of Modern American Prose Literature* (New York, 1942), 257–64; C. Hugh Holman, "Ellen Glasgow and the Southern Literary Tradition," in *Southern Writers: Appraisals in Our Time,* ed. R. C. Simonini, Jr. (Charlottesville, 1964), 103–23; J. R. Raper, *Without Shelter: The Early Career of Ellen Glasgow* (Baton Rouge, 1971); and Edward Wagenknecht, *Cavalcade of the American Novel: From the Birth of the Nation to the Middle of the Twentieth Century* (New York, 1952), 267–80. See also E. Stanly Godbold, Jr., *Ellen Glasgow and the Woman Within* (Baton Rouge, 1972).

however, in discussing two of these novels in particular—*The Battle-Ground* (1902) and *Barren Ground* (1925). These two books show the ways in which the subject of Glasgow's history and her attitudes toward that history moved the form of her novels steadily from the historical romance to the realistic social novel.[10]

Like the generation of southern writers who followed her, most notably Thomas Wolfe and William Faulkner, Ellen Glasgow was complexly ambivalent in her attitude toward the South. "I had grown up in the yet lingering fragrance of the old South," she wrote in *A Certain Measure,* "and I loved its imperishable charm, even while I revolted from its stranglehold on the intellect. Like the new South, I had inherited the tragic conflict of types." However ambivalent her feelings toward her region may have been, in her prefaces, letters, and discussions with friends she was thoroughly consistent in her distaste for the Southern Tradition in fiction:

> It was not that I disliked legend. On the contrary, I still believe that a heroic legend is the noblest creation of man. But I believe also that legend to be a blessing must be re-created not in funeral wreaths, but in dynamic tradition, and in the living character of a race.[11]

In *A Certain Measure* Glasgow defines herself as a realist, but not a member of the "American school of refined realism" of which she saw William Dean Howells as "acting dean." She asserts, "I had not revolted from the Southern sentimental fallacy in order to submit myself to the tyranny of the Northern genteel tradition." Nor, she adds, was she interested in the sort of realism that had "so often degenerated into literary ruffianism." In her most succinct statement of what she means by realism, Glasgow declares, "The true realists . . . must illuminate experience, not merely transcribe it." For Glasgow, this illumination of experience provided room for the historical and mythological dimension of Virginia in her depiction of southern life. Indeed, she contends in her preface to *The Miller of Old Church* that the South and the historical idea of the South are inseparable:

---

10. Most of Glasgow's later novels are comedies of manners. These include *The Romantic Comedians* (1926), *They Stooped to Folly* (1929), *The Sheltered Life* (1932), and *In This Our Life* (1941).

11. Glasgow, *A Certain Measure,* 12.

The old South, genial, objective, and a little ridiculous—as the fashions of the past are always a little ridiculous to the present—has vanished from the world of fact to reappear in the permanent realm of fable. This much we have already conceded. What we are in danger of forgetting is that few possessions are more precious than a fable that can no longer be compared with a fact. The race that inherits a heroic legend must have accumulated an inexhaustible resource of joy, beauty, love, laughter, and tragic passion. To discard this rich inheritance in the pursuit of a standard utilitarian style is, for the Southern novelist, pure folly.[12]

After two rather unsuccessful novels, *The Descendant* (1897) and *Phases of an Inferior Planet* (1898), which Glasgow admits were attempts "to build a philosophy of experience upon the firm theory of evolution," and following her first Virginia novel, *The Voice of the People* (1900), about post-Reconstruction politics and the ascent of the poor white class, Ellen Glasgow published her only Civil War novel, *The Battle-Ground*.[13] In spite of her claims for the realism of her antebellum society, it is difficult to find fault with Louis Rubin's assessment that "her prewar society is properly romantic, her plantation belles glamorous, her Confederate soldiers cavaliers all." Yet in her 1938 preface to the novel Glasgow declares, "I could detect no flaw in the verisimilitude of the picture." Her avowed purpose in the novel was "to portray the last stand in Virginia of the aristocratic tradition." Further on in the preface, she gives the reader an idea of why this is a difficult undertaking for a realist:

If I have dealt with the spirit of romance, it is because one cannot approach the Confederacy without touching the very heart of romantic tradition. It is the single occasion in American history, and one of the rare occasions in the history of the world, when the conflict of actualities was profoundly romantic. For Virginia, in that disastrous illusion, the Confederacy was the expiring gesture of chivalry.[14]

The Battle-Ground centers on two aristocratic Virginia families, the Lightfoots of "Chericoke" and the Amblers of "Uplands." In large measure the novel is a love story of Dan Montjoy and Betty Ambler, and it

12.   *Ibid.*, 14, 15, 142–43.
13.   *Ibid.*, 59.
14.   Rubin, "The Image of an Army," 58; Glasgow, *A Certain Measure*, 6, 13, 24–25.

moves in many predictable and expected ways. Dan is the son of Major Lightfoot's daughter, whom the major disinherited when she eloped with Montjoy, a violent man of a lower social station. At the beginning of the novel Dan's mother has died, and the sixteen-year-old boy has left his father. He arrives penniless and hungry at Chericoke. The major welcomes him into the family and raises him as an equal along with the major's nephew, Champe. Although as the major's grandson, Dan is deserving of this attention, the boy is troubled by what he calls the "Montjoy blood" in his character and often describes himself as only half a Lightfoot. His Lightfoot lineage is the inheritance of civilized gentility, but Dan fears the Montjoy violence of his other side. J. R. Raper has labeled this theme in the novel as "the psychological consequence of heredity." [15] It is only through the experience of the war and meeting his father again that Dan is freed from this schizophrenic view of his own character.

Fully half of *The Battle-Ground* is devoted to establishing the way of life of the antebellum Virginia aristocracy. Glasgow's depictions of manners, dress, and attitudes, often on ceremonial occasions such as balls and Christmas celebrations, evoke a romantic era of grace and splendor reminiscent of the moonlight-and-magnolia writers. After a brief infatuation with the other Ambler sister, Dan, a handsome and rebellious young man, recognizes his love for the sprightly, red-haired Betty. Their courtship is a series of elegant and amusing repartees.

Yet within this gallant and gentle society are the seeds of its impending collapse. Major Lightfoot, a lovable, blustering, and kindhearted gentleman, is a rabid secessionist as well. Governor Ambler, a staunch Unionist and a man with a clear-eyed vision of the dangers of the South's political course, is ineffectual in his attempts to bring his neighbor to reason. In the numerous polite arguments between the major and the governor, Glasgow hints that it is precisely because of politeness and manners that the cool heads of the South could not thwart the secessionist impulse. The rules of this courtly society are responsible for its downfall.

As a prelude to his entering the war, Dan is disinherited by the major after participating in a duel over a barmaid. There is an inherent irony, however, in Dan's plight. Though Dan considers himself "a beggar" and

15. Raper, *Without Shelter*, 173.

takes employment as a stagecoach driver, he does so with an offer to study law with a prominent judge to back him up, with his servant Big Abel at his side, and with a large complement of rich clothes and possessions. Whatever pose Dan may choose, Glasgow makes it clear that after his association with the Lightfoot name the rest of southern society will never let him return to the state of the penniless boy who arrived at the gates of Chericoke. His social standing makes his rebellion little more than a working holiday.

It is in the second half of the book, devoted to the actual war and its effects on southern society, that Glasgow's claims for the novel's realism are justified. Though her scenes of battle are few, what Glasgow does show of the war, and particularly of camp life, is the result of her research in journals, diaries, and newspapers of the period and her own visits to the locations she describes.[16] In their detail and their evocation of atmosphere, her battle scenes are reminiscent of *The Red Badge of Courage*.

In his first experience in battle, Dan finds out how thin the coverings of civilization and culture really are. The violence of his "Montjoy blood" rises to the surface. Glasgow's description is significant:

> As he bent to fire, the fury of the game swept over him and aroused the sleeping brute within him. All the primeval instincts, throttled by the restraint of centuries—the instincts of bloodguiltiness, of hot pursuit, of the fierce exhilaration of the chase, of the death grapple with a resisting foe—these awoke suddenly to life and turned the battle scarlet to his eyes.[17]

Afterward he is overcome with nausea, but his schooling in war has begun. Through his participation in the conflict Dan comes to learn that there are no real gentlemen, only men, and that men are sometimes less human than they would wish to be. Dan comes to agree with Governor Ambler that "the best, or the worst of it, is that after the first fight it comes easy . . . it comes too easy." Dan's education in the discrepancies between the world of Chericoke and the "real" world of the war is furthered by his companionship with Pinetop, an illiterate mountaineer. In his association with Pinetop, Dan confronts for the first time the true evils of the class system:

16. For an account of Glasgow's sources, see *A Certain Measure*, 19–21.
17. Ellen Glasgow, *The Battle-Ground* (New York, 1902), 312.

For the first time in his life he was brought face to face with the tragedy of hopeless ignorance for an inquiring mind, and the shock stunned him, at the moment, past the power of speech. . . . Beside that genial plantation life which he had known he saw rising the wistful figure of the poor man doomed to conditions which he could not change—born, it may be, like Pinetop, self-poised, yet with an untaught intellect, grasping, like him, after the primitive knowledge which should be the birthright of every child. . . . [Y]et these were the men who, when Virginia called, came from their little cabins in the mountains, who tied the flint-locks upon their muskets and fought uncomplainingly until the end.[18]

Dan learns to live in rage, to steal, to eat "nigger-food," to suffer pain, and finally, to be one in a group of men. In her preface to *The Battle-Ground,* Glasgow writes, "Nothing in my inquiries into the past had interested me more than the democratic feeling in the Army of Northern Virginia."[19] For Glasgow, democracy was perhaps the most valuable lesson that the South was to learn from the war.

After the Appomattox surrender, Dan is able to make his own peace with the experience of the war:

Despite the grim struggle and the wasted strength, despite the impoverished land and the nameless graves that filled it, despite even his own wrecked youth and the hard-fought fields where he had laid it down—despite all these a shadow was lifted from his people and it was worth the price.[20]

This shadow, of course, is the slave system and the class system of the Old South. Dan returns home to find Chericoke burned and the major welcoming but unregenerate; he gives himself over to the care of Betty, who in her own way has also come to terms with the experience of war. With Betty, Dan finds the strength to take up the struggle to rebuild their lives and, metaphorically at least, the South.

In her posthumously published memoir, *The Woman Within* (1954), Glasgow writes of Hamlin Garland: "His first volume of stories, *Main-Travelled Roads,* showed an almost savage fidelity to life."[21] Certainly there

18. *Ibid.,* 315, 442–43.
19. Glasgow, *A Certain Measure,* 21–22.
20. Glasgow, *The Battle-Ground,* 485.
21. Ellen Glasgow, *The Woman Within* (New York, 1954), 141.

are resonances of the ending of Garland's "The Return of a Private" in a passage near the end of *The Battle-Ground* that describes the situation Dan and Betty face at the end of the war:

> For a country that was not he had given himself as surely as the men who were buried where they fought, and his future would be but one long struggle to adjust himself to conditions in which he had no part. . . . The army was not the worst, he knew this now. . . . [T]he worst was what came afterward, this sense of utter failure and the attempt to shape one's self to brutal necessity. In the future that opened before him he saw only a terrible patience which would perhaps grow into a second nature as the years went on.[22]

In an oft-quoted passage from *A Certain Measure,* Glasgow asserts that "the South needed blood and irony"—blood because it had "strained too far away from its roots in the earth" and irony because it was "the safest antidote to sentimental decay."[23] Blood and irony are the characteristics that Dan and Betty possess, and indeed will need to possess in their grapple with Reconstruction. They are left to face the world with blood and irony, not with optimism; yet the sense is, at the end of the novel, that if courage and realism are the requirements of that facing, Glasgow's desentimentalized couple may make their way in the New South.

In *The Battle-Ground* Glasgow uses the romantic mythologies of the Old South to show that it was the romantic chauvinism of that culture that brought its downfall upon itself. On his return home from the war, Dan is fed by a woman whose son died in Pickett's Charge at Gettysburg. "My God! it was worth living to die like that," is Dan's consoling remark to the woman. "And it is worth living to have a son die like that," the woman affirms.[24] Glasgow's attitude here is clearly ironic. As the ending of the novel makes clear, those who remain living will need to leave such romance to the dead and to forge a new world out of defeat. To live still within the romance is to become like Mrs. Blake in Glasgow's *The Deliverance* (1904), who exists completely in a dream world of the undefeated

---

22. Glasgow, *The Battle-Ground,* 492–93.
23. Glasgow, *A Certain Measure,* 28.
24. Glasgow, *The Battle-Ground,* 497.

Confederacy while her children try to protect her from the realities of Reconstruction.

The progression from romance to realism in *The Battle-Ground* is also a view of history from antebellum to Reconstruction society. History becomes an evolutionary rather than a cyclical force, a progression of a culture through time rather than the preservation of the past in the present. With such a view of history, the historical imagination becomes again a dynamic force in fiction, but the method of expression of that imagination moves from the romantic to the realistic.

Glasgow has written that "with the possible exception of Dorinda Oakley in *Barren Ground,* Betty Ambler has been the best liked of my heroines. . . . For the South at least, she seemed to personify the spirit that fought with gallantry and gaiety, and that in defeat remained undefeated." Certainly Betty's heroism has its parallels in Dorinda Oakley's. Glasgow sums up the "implicit philosophy" of *Barren Ground* as being that "one may learn to live, one may even learn to live gallantly, without delight."[25] Dorinda is the inheritor of the post-Reconstruction South. Her story, which takes place between 1894 and 1924, is an account of the reformation of the class structure in Virginia. Glasgow's description of this class structure is worth quoting in full:

> The tenant farmers, who had flocked after the ruin of war as buzzards after a carcass, had immediately picked the featureless landscape as clean as a skeleton. When the swarming was over only three of the larger farms at Pedlar's Mill remained undivided in the hands of their original owners. Though Queen Elizabeth County had never been one of the aristocratic regions of Virginia, it was settled by sturdy English yeomen, with a thin but lively sprinkling of the persecuted Protestants of other nations. Several of these superior pioneers brought blue blood in their veins as well as the vigorous fear of God in their hearts; but the greater number arrived, as they remained, "good people," a comprehensive term, which implies, to discriminating Virginians, the exact opposite of the phrase, "a good family." The good families of the state have preserved, among other things, custom, history, tradition, romantic fiction, and the Episcopal Church. The good people, according to the records of clergymen, which are the only surviving records, have preserved nothing except themselves. Ignored

---

25. Glasgow, *A Certain Measure,* 5, 155.

alike by history and fiction, they have their inconspicuous place in the social strata midway between the lower gentility and the upper class of "poor white," a position which encourages the useful rather than the ornamental public virtues.

Dorinda Oakley is from a "land poor" family of "good people" of pioneer stock. The family farm is "Old Farm," "a thousand acres of scrub pine, scrub oak, and broomsedge, where a single cultivated corner was like a solitary island in some chaotic sea." Dorinda's father is described as "a slave to the land, harnessed to the elemental forces, struggling inarticulately against the blight of poverty and the barrenness of the soil." [26] Dorinda's mother is a pioneer woman whose strength comes from her devotion to the teachings of the Presbyterian Church.

In contrast to the Oakleys are the Ellgoods who, on the basis of a small inheritance and progressive farming methods, have managed to make "Green Acres" a thrifty but productive farm. The purely aristocratic family, the Greylocks, consist now only of an old alcoholic doctor, who lives with his black serving woman and the mulatto bastards he has fathered by her, and the doctor's son, Jason, a young doctor who has recently returned to Pedlar's Mill to care for his father, whom he believes to be dying. The Greylock estate, "Five Oaks," has been left to revert to scrub pine and broom sedge.

The land is the metaphor of the accomplishments of these families. The Ellgoods' farm is rich in pasture and alfalfa, and every year more land is reclaimed and put into use. Old Farm, in spite of Joshua Oakley's dogged exertions, is slowly being overrun by broom sedge. Five Oaks has not been farmed in years and is completely wild. The two dominant social groups—pioneer descendants such as the Oakleys and aristocrats such as the Greylocks—are fading out of the social structure of Pedlar's Mill. For reasons inherent in their own social character, both groups are unable to survive in their contemporary world—the aristocracy because of their inherent weaknesses, the pioneer descendants because of their ignorant distrust of new ideas, which has led them to wear out the soil with tobacco. Only a few "good people" (such as the Ellgoods) and the merchant class and the industrious blacks seem able to adjust to the changing conditions of the South.

26. Ellen Glasgow, *Barren Ground* (Garden City, N.Y., 1925), 5, 7, 40.

The success Dorinda eventually achieves is, on one level, the result of her ability to impose her will upon historical forces. Her youthful infatuation with and seduction by Jason Greylock is a result of her idealization of his weaknesses into romantic nobility. She is enraptured by his words, his appearance, and his idealism. He is, to her, the symbol of everything the Oakleys are not. When Jason betrays the pregnant Dorinda by weakly allowing himself to be pressured into marriage to Geneva Ellgood, Dorinda runs away to New York where, after losing Jason's child by a miscarriage, she learns to take control of her life and to survive in that alien setting. It is during her years in New York Dorinda is able to break free of the influence of historical forces that controlled her life at Pedlar's Mill. She develops the emotional and psychological fortitude that will make her a survivor in the world that crushes her father and Jason. She also learns to use the "instinct for survival" that she has inherited from her father and mother. When she realizes that her fate is somehow tied to the land her relatives settled, she returns home. She takes over operations at Old Farm and eventually, through intelligence, fortitude, and will, rebuilds it and acquires Five Oaks, which Jason, helplessly alcoholic and alone after Geneva's suicide, has lost to taxes.

Barren Ground is divided into three sections: "Broomsedge," "Pine," and "Life-Everlasting." The "Broomsedge" section details Dorinda's affair with Jason Greylock and her New York experiences; "Pine" chronicles her victorious struggle with the land, her sterile marriage to Nathan Pedlar, and her "revenge" on Jason through her acquisition of Five Oaks; "Life-Everlasting" narrates Dorinda's middle-aged years (forty-two to fifty) and her adoption of and caring for the debilitated Jason. Broom sedge, pine, and life-everlasting also have symbolic uses throughout the novel. Broom sedge is the botanical "fate" of the land and its inhabitants. The harp-shaped pine that grows out of the Oakley graveyard is a symbol of the hardiness and richness of Dorinda's pioneer heritage. Life-everlasting, along with its obvious rhetorical value, is a symbol of peace and beauty on an otherwise blighted landscape.

These three natural symbols, coupled with the sections named after them, intertwine into a complex theory of history in the novel, with broom sedge as the trap of the southern past, pine as a richness of the past that is translated into the present, and life-everlasting as a promise for the future. In "Broomsedge" Glasgow shows how the social structure of the Old South and its heritage has doomed the Oakleys and the Grey-locks to a steady decline in the post-Reconstruction South. "Pine" shows Dorinda's rejection of the idea of historical necessity and her reshaping of her heritage by her literal clearing of the broom sedge. "Pine" is ultimately about the triumph of the individual over the forces of history. "Life-Everlasting" examines Dorinda's coming to terms with her socie-ty's and her own history and gives the promise that the reconciliation will continue in the future through her stepson, John Abner.[27]

In her preface to *Barren Ground,* Glasgow comments, "While I have faithfully painted the colours of the Southern landscape, I have always known that this external *vraisemblance* was not essential to my interpre-tation of life."[28] In this assessment of the universality of Dorinda's pre-dicament as a nineteenth-century woman trying to come to terms with the modern world, Glasgow is, of course, correct. But there is more to it than that. For although Dorinda is a victim of the changing larger world, she is also a victim of a uniquely southern view of history, the idea that the past is a force that constantly impinges upon the present moment and that must be confronted, struggled with, and incorporated meaningfully into the present. Like Betty Ambler, Dorinda is in many ways an archetypal female martyr of the New South, who by her sacrifice and her fortitude brings the past into a dynamically creative, rather than destructive, relationship with the present. *The Battle-Ground* and *Barren Ground* show how the historical imagination grapples with and eventually may succeed in reshaping the past. As these two novels exemplify, the mode of that expression was becoming increasingly realistic.

As Ellen Glasgow struggled in the first quarter of the twentieth century to break the established mold of the romantic tradition in southern letters, midwesterner Willa Cather was also breaking the mold of her own lit-erary tradition—realism. One need only consider Cather's contempo-raries Theodore Dreiser, Sherwood Anderson, Floyd Dell, and Sinclair Lewis and compare her elegiac novels with their social realism to realize how wide a gap existed between Cather and her midwestern compatri-ots. In one sense Cather's progression as novelist was the inverse of Glasgow's. Alexandra Bergson's conquering of the land that defeated her

27. For a further discussion of Glasgow's use of natural symbols in *Barren Ground,* see Joan Foster Santas, *Ellen Glasgow's American Dream* (Charlottesville, 1965), 138–63.
28. Glasgow, *A Certain Measure,* 153.

father in *O Pioneers!* (1913) is, at least on the surface, much the same story as Dorinda Oakley's. By 1927, with *Death Comes for the Archbishop,* Cather was writing the historical novel that Glasgow eschewed after *The Battle-Ground.* Yet in any final analysis it should be obvious that Cather and Glasgow were working toward at least one common artistic goal— to bring the past and the present together into a meaningful and under- standable relationship. With Glasgow, the past had to be reinterpreted by the present; with Cather, however, the present needed measuring by the past.

I have suggested that much of the impulse behind the development of midwestern realism was a psychological use of the present tense by midwestern writers. Furthermore, this engagement with the present re- sulted from an idea of the Midwest as a new place, unhindered by the past and unlimited in the future. I also conjectured that the failure of midwestern society to achieve its ideal potential resulted in the social invective that dominates the work of nineteenth-century Middle Border novelists.

By the end of the first decade of the new century, two things were glaringly obvious to the midwestern writer. The Midwest was no longer "new," and populism was giving way quickly to middle-class materialism. In fiction "the revolt from the village" resulted from this realization. Following an impulse that had its roots in novels such as *The Story of a Country Town* and *Rose of Dutcher's Coolly,* the latter half of the second decade of the twentieth century was marked by an attack on the provin- cialism of the small town. Anthony Hilfer, in his fine study of this im- pulse, defines the attack in this way:

> The village was synecdoche and metaphor. The village represented what Americans thought they were, what they sometimes pretended (to them- selves as well as others) they wanted to be, and if the small town was typically American, the Midwestern small town was doubly typical. The basic civilization of America was middle class, a fact somewhat obscured in city novels that tended to treat the extremes of the very rich and the very poor to the exclusion of the middle. Even the East, dominated by its cities, usually granted the superior "Americanism" of the Middle West. Thus the Midwestern novelists of the teens and twenties could see their locale as a microcosm of the nation and, provincial bourgeoises that they

were, of the world. But their view was critical. The town was the focus of what was in actuality an over-all attack on middle-class American civilization.[29]

A two-year period saw the publication of Anderson's *Winesburg, Ohio* (1919), Dell's *Moon-Calf* (1920), and Lewis' *Main Street* (1920). Shortly, the retreat from the Midwest was on; writers moved first to the city, then to the East, and then often on to Europe—and they took many of their novels with them.

Willa Cather had preceded this retreat in her own moves from Red Cloud to Lincoln to Pittsburgh to New York, but ironically many of her novels remained at home, set in the Midwest. Certainly Cather was not given to idealization of the small town. The stories in her first collection, *The Troll Garden* (1905), especially "The Sculptor's Funeral" and "A Wagner Matinee," are as scathing in their indictment of provincialism as any of the sketches of *Winesburg, Ohio*. But by the time she finished her second novel, *O Pioneers!*, Cather had determined that the retreat, if it were to be made, was not to be made to the East but rather into the past.

In an essay, "The Novel Démeublé" (1922), Cather asserts that "the novel, for a long while, has been overfurnished" and advocates "throwing out the furniture" of fiction.

> There is a popular superstition that "realism" asserts itself in the cataloguing of a great number of material objects, in explaining mechanical processes, the methods of operating manufactories and trades, and in minutely and unsparingly describing physical sensations. But is not realism, more than it is anything else, an attitude of mind on the part of the writer toward his material, a vague indication of the sympathy and candour with which he accepts, rather than chooses, his theme?[30]

Cather distinguishes between observation, which she calls "a low part" of a writer's "equipment," and selection or simplification, which she regards as the highest: "If the novel is a form of imaginative art, it cannot be at the same time a vivid and brilliant form of journalism." Opposed to journalism in Cather's view is creation:

29. Hilfer, *The Revolt from the Village*, 4–5.
30. Willa Cather, "The Novel Démeublé," in *Not Under Forty* (New York, 1936), 43, 51, 45.

Whatever is felt upon the page without being specifically named there—
that, one might say, is created. It is the inexplicable presence of the thing
not named, of the overtone divined by the ear but not heard by it, the
verbal mood, the emotional aura of the fact or the thing or the deed, that
gives high quality to the novel or the drama, as well as to poetry itself.

Cather concludes her essay by noting that "the nursery tale, no less than
the tragedy, is killed by tasteless amplitude," and she calls upon the writer
to "leave the scene bare for the play of emotions."[31]

In its polemics this essay explains much about Cather's views of literary
form, history, and society. What she means by realism based on the individual feeling is not realism at all, but a nineteenth-century romantic
view handled with the techniques of the modern novel. Her condemnation of materialism in society is coupled with an antimaterialistic view
of art as well. As her contemporaries were investigating the complexity
of modern life, Cather was calling for an almost Thoreauvian simplification. For her, aesthetics and ethics are fused together in a system that
places the verities in opposition to complexities; truth and verisimilitude
may be at odds.

Implicit in this aesthetic doctrine is a retreat from the complex and
modern into the past; the ideal art is "as bare as the stage of a Greek
theatre."[32] It is worth noting that Cather's metaphors of empty rooms
and bare stages are reflected in the landscapes of her novels—Nebraska
prairies and New Mexico mesas.

This notion of ethical aesthetics helps to explain the progression in
Cather's use of the past in *O Pioneers!* (1913), *My Ántonia* (1918), and
The Professor's House (1925). Cather's fusion of the past with the present
became more successful the further removed her characters were from

31. *Ibid.,* 44–45, 48, 50, 51.
32. *Ibid.,* 51. Critical studies of Willa Cather abound. She was the first woman writer to be
included in *Fifteen Modern American Authors: A Survey of Research and Criticism,* ed. Jackson R. Bryer
(Durham, 1969), 23–62. Much of the Cather criticism is eccentric and, especially that dealing with
her "retreat" from realism, ill-willed. Some of the best critical assessment of Cather is to be found
in Kazin, *On Native Grounds,* 247–57; and in Louis Auchincloss, *Pioneers & Caretakers: A Study of
Nine American Women Novelists* (Minneapolis, 1965), 92–122. Indispensable is James Woodress, *Willa
Cather: Her Life and Art* (New York, 1970). Two collections of reviews and essays, *Willa Cather and
Her Critics,* ed. James Schroeter (Ithaca, 1967), and *The Art of Willa Cather,* ed. Bernice Slote and
Virginia Faulkner (Lincoln, 1974), are quite useful. See also E. K. Brown and Leon Edel, *Willa
Cather: A Critical Biography* (New York, 1953), and Elizabeth Shepley Sergeant, *Willa Cather: A
Memoir* (1953; rpr. Lincoln, 1963).

the modern world. In *O Pioneers!*, the actual land of the Great Divide is presented at its most mythic and symbolic level; the earth itself becomes a historical force that links Alexandra Bergson with the prehistory of the continent. *My Ántonia,* through the characters of Ántonia Shimerda and Jim Burden, joins the values of the world of the settler to the man of the modern world. What the modern world has lost is still recoverable through the character of Ántonia. In *The Professor's House,* the present and the values of the past are finally divided when Godfrey St. Peter succumbs to the demands of the forces of his modern world.

With the exception of the romantic tragedy of the young lovers' murder, *O Pioneers!* is the chronicle of Alexandra Bergson's relationship to the land or to what Cather frequently calls the "Spirit" or "Genius of the Divide."[33] Alexandra is both literally and figuratively "pure" in her devotion to the land. Her recurring dream is of a man—"like no man she knew," who is "yellow like the sunlight" and with "the smell of ripe cornfields about him"—who carries her "as easily as if she were a sheaf of wheat." Alexandra is united with the land:

> For the first time, perhaps, since that land emerged from the waters of geologic ages, a human face was set toward it with love and yearning. It seemed beautiful to her, rich and strong and glorious. Her eyes drank in the breadth of it, until her tears blinded her. Then the Genius of the Divide, the great, free spirit which breathes across it, must have bent lower than it ever bent to a human will before. The history of every country begins in the heart of a man or a woman.[34]

Alexandra is literally in touch with the land; she sees it as a living, dynamic force with which she communes. She succeeds, in part because of some mythic and racial understanding she has of the land, in creating a prosperous farm where her father failed. Her father saw the land only as antagonist:

> In eleven long years John Bergson had made but little impression upon the wild land he had come to tame. It was still a wild thing that had its

---

33. For a closer examination of nature in *O Pioneers!* and *My Ántonia,* see John H. Randall III, "Interpretation of *My Ántonia,*" in *Willa Cather and Her Critics,* ed. Schroeter, 272–322.
34. Willa Cather, *O Pioneers!* (Boston, 1913), 206, 65.

ugly moods; and no one knew when they were likely to come, or why. Mischance hung over it. Its Genius was unfriendly to man.[35]

Cather alludes to Alexandra's mystical communication with the land throughout the novel. In the final passage of O Pioneers! is the promise of a mystical rebirth for Alexandra when she will literally be made part of earth: the country will "receive hearts like Alexandra's into its bosom, to give them out again in the yellow wheat, in the rustling corn, in the shining eyes of youth!"[36]

The apostrophic title of the novel is not borne out in the story. The other pioneers do not live in the same relationship to the physical world as Alexandra does, and which Cather seems to value so highly. Alexandra's two older brothers share neither her communion with nor her faith in the earth. Carl, her close friend, and Emil, her cherished younger brother, both make their way into the modern world. Though he is engaged to Alexandra at the end of the novel, Carl's returns to the prairie are temporary. Emil's return is fatal, and his death seems to be some sort of blood sacrifice demanded of Alexandra by the land. Emil and Carl have lost Alexandra's simplicity, and with it the ability to communicate with the primordial Genius of the Divide.

The past of O Pioneers! is finally not the historical period of the novel, but rather a past that stretches back prehistorically and is lodged in our racial memory and in the character of Alexandra. O Pioneers! is an elegy to the irrecoverable innocence and simplicity of the American garden.

My Ántonia is structured on dichotomies—the past and the present, the town and the farm, Jim Burden and Ántonia Shimerda. The novel is Jim Burden's story, as the title implies and the introduction makes explicit. It is a story of the past, but of a personal past—Jim Burden's Ántonia. As his name implies, Jim is weighed down by the modern world, and his memories of his youth on the Nebraska prairie form a system of values in which he finds the present lacking. He is now a corporation lawyer for the railroad (traditionally the symbol of opposition to the farmer) and lives in New York with his wife, who "lives her own life" and "for some reason . . . wishes to remain Mrs. James Burden."[37]

35. Ibid., 20.
36. Ibid., 309.
37. Willa Cather, My Ántonia (Boston, 1918), xi.

This thumbnail sketch is all we know about the mature Jim Burden, because in his own narrative he wants to recapture the past, not to speak of the present. It is his prerogative as artist, but often in his narrative he shows unconsciously the present impinging upon the past. One excellent example of this comes early in the novel:

> Sometimes I followed the sunflower-bordered roads. Fuchs told me that the sunflowers were introduced into that country by the Mormons; that at the time of the persecution, when they left Missouri and struck out into the wilderness to find a place where they could worship God in their own way, the members of the first exploring party, crossing the plains to Utah, scattered sunflower seed as they went. The next summer, when the long trains of wagons came through with all the women and children, they had the sunflower trail to follow. I believe that botanists do not confirm Jake's story, but insist that the sunflower was native to those plains. Nevertheless, that legend has stuck in my mind, and sunflower-bordered roads always seem to me the roads to freedom.[38]

The knowledge of the modern world continually distances the past.

In the first section of the novel, "The Shimerdas," the country population, composed of the first settlers' families and various immigrant groups, form an egalitarian society. Jim grows up playing with Ántonia, whose family arrived in the district the same evening as the Burdens. When Jim's family moves to town and Ántonia is hired to cook at the house next door, Jim and Ántonia's relationship undergoes a subtle change, as the section title, "The Hired Girls," implies. Such distinctions, after the closeness of the families in the first section, point out the artificiality of the structure of town society. Increasingly, Jim and Ántonia are separated by social convention. He is a "Black Hawk" boy; she is a "country girl." And in the eyes of the town mothers, the country girls are a "menace to the social order."[39]

Just before Jim leaves town to study at the university in Lincoln, he goes on a picnic with the country girls. In a magnificently conceived scene, Cather presents an epiphany of the values that Jim is leaving behind in the country:

38. *Ibid.*, 31–32.
39. *Ibid.*, 229.

Just as the lower edge of the red disc rested on the high fields against the horizon, a great black figure suddenly appeared on the face of the sun. We sprang to our feet, straining our eyes toward it. In a moment we realized what it was. On some upland farm, a plough had been left standing in the field. The sun was sinking just behind it. Magnified across the distance by the horizontal light, it stood out against the sun, was exactly contained within the circle of the disc; the handles, the tongue, the share—black against the molten red. There it was, heroic in size, a picture writing on the sun.

As with the sunflowers, narrator Jim Burden cannot leave the image at its symbolic and most meaningful level. He cannot stop himself from diminishing it:

The ball dropped and dropped until the red tip went beneath the earth. The fields below us were dark, the sky was growing pale, and that forgotten plough had sunk back to its own littleness somewhere on the prairie.[40]

As Burden's narrative moves closer and closer to the present, Ántonia's place in the novel recedes. Others of the country girls move away from the district. Lena, Ántonia's and Jim's friend, moves to Lincoln and later to San Francisco. After numerous adventures another of the girls, Tiny, becomes a wealthy entrepreneur in San Francisco. When Jim sees her years later, she confides to him "that nothing interested her much now but making money."[41] The sense is that as successful as these girls become, they are also, like Jim, corrupted by the modern world.

Even the small town of Black Hawk is enough to corrupt Ántonia; she becomes pregnant by a train conductor who promises to marry her and then deserts her. In shame, Ántonia returns to the Shimerda farm and works in the fields. Later, when Jim visits her on a trip through town, she has become her old self again; she has been cleansed, metaphorically, by her contact with the earth. Even with her child, she is a "country girl" again.

As many critics have pointed out, in Burden's account of his visit with

40. *Ibid.*, 279.
41. *Ibid.*, 340.

Ántonia after a twenty-year absence, she becomes an earth-mother figure. The scenes of Ántonia with her "ten or eleven" children almost
ooze fertility. Ántonia's table, garden, and grape arbor are cornucopian.
She has become, for Jim, a symbol of the irrecoverable past:

> She lent herself to immemorial human attitudes which we recognize by
> instinct as universal and true. I had not been mistaken. She was a battered
> woman now, not a lovely girl; but she still had that something which fires
> the imagination, could still stop one's breath for a moment by a look or
> a gesture that somehow revealed the meaning in common things. She had
> only to stand in the orchard, to put her hand on a little crab tree and look
> up at the apples, to make you feel the goodness of planting and tending
> and harvesting at last. All the strong things of her heart came out in her
> body, that had been so tireless in serving generous emotions.
>
> It was no wonder that her sons stood tall and straight. She was a rich
> mine of life, like the founders of early races.[42]

Burden's final word in the novel is an elegy:

> For Ántonia and for me, this had been the road of Destiny; had taken us
> to those early accidents of fortune which predetermined for us all that we
> can ever be. Now I understood that the same road was to bring us together
> again. Whatever we had missed, we possessed together the precious, the
> incommunicable past.

Yet the elegy is only Jim's, not Ántonia's. What Jim has lost in the modern
world, Ántonia still possesses in hers. Burden has forgotten what Ántonia
told him when they parted twenty years before. When Jim promised to
return, Ántonia replied, "Perhaps you will—. . . But even if you don't,
you're here, like my father. So I won't be lonesome." [43] In living close to
the earth Ántonia has never been forced into separating the past and the
present. Instead, for her they are one. Unlike Jim's, her present is as full
as her past. Jim, the artist, can only re-create what Ántonia, the pioneer
woman, lives.

In *The Professor's House* (1925), the sense of the past that was immediate
in *O Pioneers!* and recoverable through art in *My Ántonia* is finally made

42. *Ibid.,* 398.
43. *Ibid.,* 419, 365.

unavailable to Professor Godfrey St. Peter by the pressure of the world around him. St. Peter is a man who has lived in the past for much of his adult life. He is a professor of history at a small college. He has lived in France, the home of his ancestors, and he has accepted his post at a small college in Michigan because it is close to Lake Michigan, the place of his childhood. But most importantly, he has lived with the conquistadores during his fifteen-year, eight-volume project, *Spanish Explorers in the New World.* The last two volumes of his study have brought him international acclaim and have made him the recipient of the Oxford Prize, a large cash award with which, at his wife's urging, he has bought a new home he neither needs nor desires. St. Peter suddenly has every material thing he might want, but he has lost his relationship with the past in the completion of his project. This loss is paralleled by the fact that his move to the new home will force St. Peter to leave his old study, the sanctuary in which he escaped the present and was able to recover the past through his work.

St. Peter also has lost Tom Outland, a gifted student and friend who was killed in the First World War. Before coming to college, Outland discovered the remains of an ancient civilization in New Mexico and traveled to Washington in an attempt to persuade the Smithsonian Institution to excavate the site. When his attempts failed, he returned to New Mexico to find that his partner had sold the artifacts. Refusing to touch his share of the money, Outland came to college and went on to become a physics instructor. Shortly before he went to war, Outland invented an airplane engine and willed the rights to St. Peter's older daughter who, with her husband, developed the patent into a considerable fortune.

The Professor's House is divided into three parts: "The Family," "Tom Outland's Story," and "The Professor." "The Family" relates St. Peter's life and establishes his love of history and knowledge and his opposition to his family's materialism. The professor would gladly give back his prize money if he could "[buy] back the fun [he] had writing [his] history." The second section of the novel is Outland's journal account of his discovery of the remains of the cliff dwellers' civilization. It chronicles Outland's excitement over his find and his disillusionment over what he regards as his partner's betrayal; the section ends with Outland's leaving for college. Part three, "The Professor," describes St. Peter's summer alone in his old rented house, where he has moved while his family tours Europe. During this summer of meditation the professor is able to recapture the past of his childhood, but he also suffers from severe depression. When he learns of his family's imminent return from Europe, St. Peter loses the youthful alter ego he has recovered through his meditations and, in a severe depression, cannot bring himself to flee when the gas stove in his study almost asphyxiates him. He is rescued by a chance visitor. Knowing that he can never again recover the past that made his life meaningful to himself, he is left to face the materialism of his family and the modern world:

> He had never learned to live without delight. And he would have to learn to, just as, in a Prohibition country, he supposed he would have to learn to live without sherry. Theoretically he knew that life is possible, maybe even pleasant, without joy, without passionate griefs. But it had never occurred to him that he might have to live like that.[44]

The corruption of the past and of the artist by materialism is the major theme of the novel. Both St. Peter and Outland, who never wished for wealth, are cursed with a Midas touch. The rewards of the professor's research threaten not only his removal from his study in the rented home, but also his marriage, due to his wife's newfound acquisitiveness. The Outland fortune corrupts not only St. Peter's family but also, by association, the professor himself. Money, which was not available for Outland's excavation, becomes, after his death, the legacy by which his memory lives. Cather's final irony is the professor's son-in-law's use of some of the Outland money to establish a memorial to Outland—not as the man who discovered a lost civilization, but as the man who invented the airplane engine that is worth so much. "If Outland were here to-night," the professor muses, "he might say with Mark Antony, *My fortunes have corrupted honest men.*"[45]

The Professor's House is Cather's expression of the aesthetic/ethical nightmare implied in "The Novel Démeublé." Materialism triumphs over art; modern society renders the past irrecoverable; simplicity falls victim to complexity; passion gives way to apathy. St. Peter's historical

---

44. Willa Cather, *The Professor's House* (New York, 1925), 33, 282.
45. *Ibid.,* 150.

imagination, which constantly connects history with the present moment, extinguishes itself. The sense that could find some humorous consolation in connecting his wealthy daughter's ostentatious shopping spree in Chicago with "Napoleon looting the Italian palaces" is no longer available to him.[46]

Though he has learned, like Dorinda Oakley of *Barren Ground,* to face the world without joy and without passion, St. Peter has lost "something very precious" in coming to terms with the modern world. He is indifferent to his life; he has lost his desire.

Early in the novel Cather underlines the importance of that desire: "A man can do anything if he wishes to enough, St. Peter believed. Desire is creation, is the magical element in that process." Glasgow's Dorinda Oakley, through sacrifice and will, shapes her destiny and reinterprets her history. In *The Professor's House,* Godfrey St. Peter is defeated by the forces of the modern world. Finally, sapped of his desire and his imagination, he relinquishes himself to apathy. Unlike his beloved explorers and cliff dwellers who shaped a world, St. Peter is finally and despairingly shaped by his.

> Lying on his old couch, he could almost believe himself in that house already. The sagging springs were like the sham upholstery that is put in coffins. Just the equivocal American way of dealing with serious facts, he reflected. Why pretend that it is possible to soften that last hard bed?[47]

In his study of Willa Cather's life James Woodress notes the many similarities between the lives of Cather and St. Peter, including Cather's Pulitzer Prize and her growing status as a literary celebrity.[48] Whether Cather experienced any apathetic reaction to her growing wealth and fame is not known, but after *The Professor's House* she never again attempted in a novel to fuse the modern Midwest with the past. Only two of her last five novels are set in the Midwest, and the action of these novels takes place in urban settings, Chicago and New York. The other three are retreats into the past, to the nineteenth-century Southwest in *Death Comes for the Archbishop* (1927), to seventeenth-century Quebec in

46. *Ibid.,* 154.
47. *Ibid.,* 29, 272.
48. Woodress, *Willa Cather: Her Life and Art,* 207–13.

Shadows on the Rock (1931), and to the antebellum South in *Sapphira and the Slave Girl* (1940).

Cather and Ellen Glasgow occupy similar positions in the literature of their regions. Both writers were striving to break out of the molds that had predominated in the literary expressions of their regions. For Glasgow, this meant not only throwing off the immediate Southern Tradition of the antebellum culture of Cooke and Page, but also separating herself from an entire literary tradition of the historical romance and the notion of history that tradition implied. She had to do no less than transform the notion of history as fate that had ruled southern letters and much of southern thought in the nineteenth century. As Glasgow noted, the richness of South's heroic legend could not be discarded, but rather had to be brought again into a dynamic relationship with the present. Glasgow's New South was not romantic, and the terms for expressing that section and its people demanded of her a more realistic approach than the romance could provide.

As already suggested, even in *The Battle-Ground* the romantic form of the novel changes with its subject matter. Glasgow's antebellum South is romantic, but her depiction of the Civil War and its aftermath is firmly in the realistic tradition. Glasgow does not discard mythology in her novels, nor does she refute the past; nowhere is there the sense that she believes the past to be unimportant to the present. Rather, throughout her work Glasgow's southern characters must recognize and confront the past as a force in their lives. To ignore the past is impossible, but to hide from the present is disastrous, as proves to be the case for Major Lightfoot in *The Battle-Ground* and for the Greylocks in *Barren Ground*. From the early Virginia novels to the late comedies of manners, the incompatibility of the idealized past and the imperfect present provided the situation for the dramas in almost all of Glasgow's work. The sense of the past impinging upon the present moment, and the necessity for the novelist to explore and to document and perhaps to make meaningful that intersection, never diminished in Glasgow's fiction. In this sense, Glasgow was the inheritor of the southern literary tradition that extended back to Simms.

Perhaps, as most students of Cather's work speculate at one time or another, it was her early childhood in Virginia, before her parents moved to Nebraska, that bred in her so intense a longing for the past. Or perhaps, as other critics have speculated, Cather retained throughout her life a farm girl's naïveté about modern life. But it is difficult to believe that the artist who chose to write a novel set in the South only in the twilight of her career had been so greatly influenced by those early years, or that the worldly woman journalist who spent most of her life in New York and was quite comfortable in Europe was never quite able to look the modern world squarely in the face. As James Woodress has pointed out in his critical biography, many of the sources of Cather's novels were drawn directly from her childhood and college years in Nebraska.[49] Certainly her reverence for the pioneer heritage of the Midwest came from this experience, but Cather's use of that heritage was a direct result of her communication with the modern world. Alfred Kazin has put it well:

> What she loved in the pioneer tradition was human qualities rather than institutions—the qualities of Ántonia Shimerda and Thea Kronberg [the heroine of *The Song of the Lark*], Alexandra Bergson and Godfrey St. Peter—but as those qualities seemed to disappear from the national life she began to think of them as something more than personal traits; they became the principles which she was to oppose to contemporary dissolution.[50]

Most of Cather's heroes and heroines are either pioneers and farmers or artists. As such they are in touch with elemental forms of beauty that guide and instruct them. Cather's reaction against the realism of her predecessors and her peers was a reaction against what she probably saw as indictment without instruction. Certainly Cather was as much in the legion against provincialism and injustice as Joseph Kirkland, Howe, and Garland were, and equally as vigorously the opponent of narrow-mindedness and materialism as Anderson, Dell, and Lewis. In fact, in her outrage at the unfulfilled promise of her region and at the pawning of the region's future by modern society, Cather was perhaps the most midwestern of them all. But there was in Cather, unlike her contemporaries, the belief that the values lost in the past might somehow provide a promise for the future. At bottom she was, like the long line of midwestern writers who preceded and succeeded her, a lecturer, a moralist, and a social critic.

In *The Woman Within,* Ellen Glasgow declares, "My social history had

49. *Ibid., passim.*
50. Kazin, *On Native Grounds,* 250.

sprung from a special soil, and it could grow and flower, naturally, in no other air." [51] Willa Cather could make the same claim for *O Pioneers!, My Ántonia,* and *The Professor's House.* Certainly Glasgow and Cather, leaving out regional considerations, have made lasting contributions to American letters, as have Simms, Garland, and Cable. In the novels of Glasgow and Cather is a pervasive sense of place; the work of both is of America, but of different Americas. All are novels in which their characters confront a changing world, but those worlds and the changes within them are different for each novelist. Glasgow's southerners and Cather's midwesterners, like their authors, are from different regions and cultures, and they face their dilemmas with attitudes and values that result from different pasts and different attitudes toward history, from different social structures and different social customs, from vastly different landscapes and very different lives.

Earlier I cited Hamlin Garland's definition of regional literature, "a literature as no other locality could produce, a literature that could not have been written in any other time, or among other surroundings." [52] I have attempted to show that "locality" and "surroundings," region and the psychology of region, can be as important an aspect as the concept of time in our understanding of American literature and the direction it has taken. Certainly time is our most convenient category for the organization of literary history. Over time we can see patterns emerge in literary form, theme, and subject. But such categorization points mainly to similarities, and often it does not account for, or else ignores, the differences that create the richness of American letters. Such patterns can show the similarities between William Gilmore Simms and Nathaniel Hawthorne, between Caroline Kirkland and John Pendleton Kennedy, between Ellen Glasgow and Willa Cather, and may even point to some of the differences. But I would argue that it is locality and surroundings, much more than time, that constitute the impulses and impetuses behind the artist's creation of the work itself, and often behind the form that the work takes. The study of American literature and the study of regional letters are not separate activities; rather, taken together, they are integral to our understanding of the literature our country has produced.

51. Glasgow, *The Woman Within,* 195.
52. Garland, "Provincialism," in *Crumbling Idols,* 26.

5

A Narrowing Distance, a Widening Gyre: Region and Modernism

If Willa Cather exhibits a break from the social realism of her predecessors and her contemporaries—Anderson, Lewis, Dell, and
Dreiser—she nonetheless appears more closely aligned with those writers
than with the next generation of midwestern writers, most notably Ernest Hemingway and F. Scott Fitzgerald. And if Ellen Glasgow was seek-
ing a new way of bringing the romantic southern past into line with a
"realistic" contemporary world, she still reminds us more of the school
of George W. Cable than of the production of William Faulkner. Although Glasgow embraced many ideas that were inimical to the nineteenth-century belief in the dualism of Good and Evil, particularly the
social Darwinism of her earlier novels, still there lingers in the work of
this Virginia woman the overpowering sense of the providence of merit,
a reward for that "vein of iron," as Glasgow termed Presbyterian stoicism.

Though these two writers were in the forefront of the literary revolutions of their regions, and continued to write and to produce some of their best work well into the 1930s, their artistic sensibilities were shaped more by the conventions of the turn of the century than by the radical new way of seeing the world that characterized modernist literature of both the United States and Great Britain.

Modernism was to a great extent a rebellion against the Victorian mind and the literary traditions it had cherished. For the English literary activist Wyndham Lewis, as for many others, the enemy was romanticism, the belief that the source of knowledge rested within the individual and that the world was constantly and personally re-created by the individual mind, which had personal access to universal truths. Balanced with the rejection of romantic thought was the rejection of the often unstructured form of poetry and the eschewing of the romance form in fiction. Modernist theorists called for a new literature, one that did not rely so much upon individual perception of the truth, but rather upon the individual's knowledge of his society and culture. Modernist verse is difficult poetry, often obscure in allusion and certainly elitist in education. Some poets rejected the romantic tradition and harked back to the difficult, controlled forms of the metaphysical poets and to eighteenth-century critical thought. As a result, this new poetry became a way of connecting the modern world with the world that had gone before, and the poets attempted through verse, as Donne had, to link two or more separate moments or ideas while creating a tension that reinforced the central idea of the work itself. Though the modernist call to arms was first sounded in Great Britain, American poets quickly enlisted and, taking their lead from their British compatriots, sought to bring this new verse form to its highest level. It was perhaps because of the felt need to hark back to a tradition, or else to break away from one, that the three most difficult practitioners of that verse were Americans—midwesterner T. S. Eliot, southerner Allen Tate, and westerner Ezra Pound.

But the call from the modernist camp was not merely one of aesthetics. Instead, an aesthetic had resulted from the experiences of the contemporary world, a world indelibly altered by the events of the second decade of the twentieth century. Virginia Woolf's famous declaration that "on or about December, 1910, human character changed" was as accurate in its hyperbole for American writers as it was for Woolf's British colleagues.

The "Great War" that entangled Europe and America from July 28, 1914, to November 11, 1918, only bore out the defeat of a culture whose demise had been noted by Woolf and others years earlier.

As Leah Watkins has pointed out, the principal element of modernist literature is the fragment, the single historical moment in which the forces of culture and society collide into the meaningful ordinary. In other words, the single instance, selected for its representative ordinariness, stands for the entire history of the culture and its civilization behind it. The fragment is metaphorical in nature, but it is not simply metaphor; the moment exists of itself and stands for nothing except in its relation to the world of which it is the culmination—something akin to Eliot's definition of the "objective correlative." This idea of the fragment is clearly seen in the barroom of *The Waste Land* or the twenty-four hours of *Ulysses* and is perhaps best exemplified by Joyce's use of the epiphany, that single moment in which all history and culture seem to coalesce into knowledge.

The relationship of modernist thinking to the events of World War I has been the focus of many critical inquiries. It has been perhaps most completely explored by Paul Fussell in *The Great War and Modern Memory,* yet a few points bear some remark here. What the war showed to the world, and by extension to its writers, was the failure of human society to accomplish the values on which it had rested its assumptions of the way the world worked. Poison gas, trench warfare, casualties in the hundreds of thousands in a single campaign, the loss of the idea of war as a system of honor, the loss of the chivalric myth of personal combat to the impersonal carnage of artillery and grenades—all these horrors showed a new world terrifying in its pronouncement of the failure of that society and its age, and raised questions about the assumptions of modern progress that would have baffled a prewar Victorian. That "God was on our side," a fact not to be doubted in 1913, was not so smugly a part of the consciousness of the man of 1918. The notion of a merciful and controlling God was severely tested, and for many destroyed, by the mass slaughter of the Battle of the Somme and the horrors of Verdun.

But the most important assumption to fall victim to the first "modern war" was more fundamental even than the belief in the infallibility of God and country; that assumption concerned the nature of history in Western culture. Much of the nineteenth century (and the eighteenth as well) believed in a concept of history best described by G. W. F. Hegel in *Reason in History*. This concept held as its implicit premise that history is linear and proceeding toward the Good; in other words, history is a continuum in which man and his society are perforce tending toward the better. For Hegel, this continuum was the result of dynamic conflict between forces (*thesis* and *antithesis* in his terms), which results in a synthesis that will bring a new and higher order. This theory is somewhat like the idea of Shakespearean tragedy, but with a convincingly happy ending. Hegel was not so much inventing a theory of history as he was echoing the philosophic idealism of his century. In 1913, one did not need to have read Hegel in order to believe that the future held a promise greater than the past (unless, of course, one was a southerner). For a generation of writers the events of World War I brought those assumptions of ideal history into question and often to rejection, just as the events of World War I would bring another "lost" generation to try to come to terms with still another example of history gone bad.

So fundamental a change in thinking, of course, had significant, complex, and lasting effects on the individual artists who tried to communicate the silent way in which the planet had cracked and the orb had shattered.

Yet the modernist position on literature was never just a political, philosophical, or aesthetic affair, and it would be a great mistake to overstate the case for World War I as the cause of this new movement in the arts. Modernism had many sources: the inadequacy of idealistic philosophy to present a world recognizable as the present, the failure of romantic assumptions to describe the twentieth-century world, the failure of romantic literature to reestablish the individual within the greater culture, the fear of the "uncultured" reader, the discord throughout Europe and the rising socialist tendencies in Britain and America, and new scientific discoveries that brought visible changes in the ways of life of the world's people. Of equal importance was the discovery by literary artists of the theories of Sigmund Freud and Carl Jung, which brought with it the assumption of an inner landscape directly related to the outer one. And it was with such relationships that the modernist was concerned: man to culture, culture to history, art to philosophy, the inner world to the outer, the present world to the world before. Modernist artists tried to find the perspective (and perspective is what marked the change in painting of this period, just as a new view of proportion marked the changes in sculpture) that could most clearly, albeit complexly, present these relationships. The modernist writer found himself described well by Virginia Woolf's character Bernard in *The Waves* as seeing himself as "a fin in a waste of water" and trying to explain his relationship to that bleak seascape.

Thus it was that the modernist found himself breaking away from the literary assumptions of realism and romanticism by ironically synthesizing many of the premises of romantic literature and realism. On one hand the modernists eschewed the "soft-minded" Promethean ideal of the romantic poets, and at the same time they found a new way of extending the individual into the entirety of history and culture through the use of the fragment. They rejected the easy, sweeping moralizations of realism, claiming that any such universal ideas could not be borne out in the world that art confronts. Yet as they glanced somewhat askance at George Eliot and William Dean Howells, they were themselves a generation of activist writers whose intent in showing the world "as it is," one suspects, had in it the implicit idealism of the world as it could be. At once they remind us of the romantics in their use of myth and of the modern existentialists in their rejection of any all-encompassing deity. For the modernists there could be no universal or everlasting idea, but only its individual substitute in Molly Bloom's "Yes" at the end of *Ulysses*. They found themselves within a paradox; they were at once romantics without a faith, nihilists with a purpose—and it is that basic irony, and the tension it produces, that distinguish modernism from the literary movements that preceded it. Thus, they could use metaphor as a form of symbol, a pattern that perhaps explains the modernist poets' affinity for the metaphysicals. History was a metaphor for the life of the individual, and the life of the individual was in some ways symbolic of the history of his culture. The fragment was metaphor for this ironic tension between the individual and his world, and at the same time no more than what insistently it was—a fragment.

The modernists' position on the inadequacy of the literature of the previous century, and their own experiments with elements of narration and time, led to another distinguishing characteristic—namely, the concept that literary form is inseparable from literary content. Given as subject matter the description of a world in which so much appeared to

have gone awry, and given the fact that science, the same force so responsible for World War I's horrible toll in lives, had pushed the idea of
God further and further toward the recesses of the universe and thus
further from and even more inaccessible to man's belief, form therefore
became of primary importance. Without their concern with form, the
modernists must psychologically have feared that their work would surrender to Victorian moralizing or else would fall apart from its inherent
dissociation. Form, then, became a way, to borrow from *The Waste Land,*
of allowing these writers to "shore against their ruins." And with their
belief in the inadequacy of previous literature to explain the modern
world, that concern with form must necessarily lead to experimentation.

The modernist dilemma provided the midwestern and the southern
writer with new ways of confronting the old regional ideologies. To the
midwesterner the inherent assumption that the world was not fulfilling
its promise was a tenet of the republicanism the region had always pro-
fessed. For the southern writer, the "new-found" necessity of linking
the past and the present within the single moment in order to make sense
of the world had been an aspect of the southern psyche ever since the
defeat of the Lost Cause. That perhaps the two most important American
post–World War I fiction writers, southerner William Faulkner and midwesterner Ernest Hemingway, eagerly embraced the call of modernism
was almost inevitable when one considers the basic cultural assumptions
of their respective regions. The Sartrean prescription for the artist to
present the world in such a way that he can live with that world was no
revelation to the writers of either the South or the Midwest. Indeed, that
had been the focus of regional writing since the advent of realism. But
if the similarities were great, the differences were greater. If the distance
between regions had narrowed, the gyre had widened.

The surprising artistic achievement of William Faulkner or Thomas
Wolfe, which might at first seem to present a break with the southern
literary tradition that preceded them, also shares the basic characteristics
of southern fiction from William Gilmore Simms onward. The novels of
these two writers, particularly those of Faulkner, though they may concern the haunted mind of a single character, also present within the story
of the individual the history of the southern people. In this sense *Absalom,
Absalom!* is, like *The Yemassee,* an epic story; it is the history of a region,
its people and its heritage. It is an attempt to formulate the mythos that

can bring the post–World War I South into a meaningful relationship
with the past. To a greater extent than any previous southern writer,
Faulkner exhibits the historical imagination at its fullest; for in his fiction
we see, perhaps more than in the work of any other American writer,
the desperate necessity of creating a heritage that will shape both
Souths—the Old and the New—into something that can simultaneously
support both the search for meaning and the intellectual despair of the
modern southerner. A heritage, for Faulkner, is something that can be
believed in, because believing in nothing, or its existential equivalent, is
not an option available to the historical imagination of the modern inheritor of those southern ghosts and avatars, of that southern blood-
knowledge of tragedy and defeat.

Nowhere is this necessity clearer than in *The Sound and the Fury* (1929),
which depicts the failure of its modern southern characters to come to
terms with their history and heritage. Benjy is clearly trapped within
history, the idiot savant who can sense the truth but cannot put it into a
framework of cognition. Frozen in time, unable to make clear distinctions
between the past and the present, Benjy acts out, at its most basic, the
terrifying trap of not differentiating the past from the present. His in-
ability to distinguish and thereby to understand the difference between
"his" pasture and the present-day golf course leaves him in a sheltered
hell reminiscent of that of Mrs. Lightfoot, the old blind woman in Ellen
Glasgow's *The Deliverance,* who believes the South has remained un-
changed and unconquered since her antebellum childhood. In his re-
tarded innocence Benjy is a character who pointedly reminds the reader
of the trap of the romantic notion of the innocent savage, for although
the idiot is comfortable with what he knows, he does not know enough
to survive the test of making meaning in the modern world. "Caddy
smelled like trees" is at once Benjy's all-embracing truth and his failure
to see the world from a knowledge born of experience. And it is precisely
that experience and its internalization that constitute for Faulkner the
real "vale of soul-making." Attractive as he may be to our romantic notions of innocence, Benjy is finally cut off from any interaction with the
external world and, no longer a force or consciousness, becomes rather
the unheard, irrelevant voice of the asylumed castrate.

In Faulkner's magnificent irony, Caddy is, in at least one fundamental
way, the obverse of Benjy. Caddy is clearly one of Faulkner's "modern

women." Though not a bitch-goddess like Miss Rosa of *Absalom, Absalom!* or Drusilla of *The Unvanquished,* Caddy's impatience with convention and tradition places her in close philosophical proximity to Brett Ashley of Hemingway's *The Sun Also Rises.* Like Benjy, Caddy is trapped by the past—not like her brother, who is trapped in a moment, but rather in the psychology of a history at once brutal, tragic, and romantic. We do not need the overt irony of Faulkner's later chronology of the Compsons, in which Caddy is reported seen in the company of German generals of World War II, to tell us that whatever future cause she might ally herself with will be as lost as that of the homeland of her childhood.

Caddy's brother Quentin is of course the complex character, the southern intellectual who tries through knowledge to deny his heritage, only to fall prey to it in the most facile fashion. Quentin's desire to step outside time and his occult psychological infatuation with his sister's "honor" as defined by her virginity show within him the dual and complex southern tendency to attempt to deny the past and yet to be helplessly and, in this case, tragically held by the underpinnings of the South's cultural assumptions. Like Caddy, he cannot successfully bridge the past and the present; in his desire to negate the past, he ignores the hold it has upon him in the present. When he reaches his epiphany, when from the bridge he sees the fish in the water and translates it into the plight of all modern men, he fails to see that that plight is filtered through a southern psyche, and that the questions that are so meaningful to his romantically existential Harvard friends are inadequate to alleviate the urgency of his southern imagination, which, for all its posturing, still believes in and must always be in thrall to the past as well as the present. Albert Camus, that romantically existential philosopher, once commented that the first and therefore only philosophical question is whether or not to commit suicide. Yet Quentin has no such modern motive for his actions. His suicide is not a rejection of the past, but rather a demented affirmation of the power of that past upon him. To ignore the pull of history and the necessity to achieve peace with the past in order to make the present meaningful is to be destroyed not by the world, but literally and symbolically by one's own hand. It is of Quentin, more than anyone else in the novel, that the phrase "signifying nothing" (conjured by the novel's title) is descriptive.

Jason Compson, Faulkner's "modern" man, offers no such solution.

Jason is able, to a greater degree than any other Compson male, to look at the world as a realist and to see it for what it is. And yet he is the character perhaps best understood in his clarity and most deplorable in his humanity. Having given up the abstractions, the values that Faulkner often litanizes—love and honor, pity and pride, compassion and sacrifice—Jason sees himself as complete, and undifferentiated from what he does and how he acts. One suspects that Jason would be Faulkner's addition to the doomed existential characters of Sartre's *No Exit,* whose hell is to confront themselves forever in terms of their actions rather than their intentions. But Faulkner has sympathy for Jason as well as condemnation, because Jason is the character most cognizant of the dilemma of history; his recognition of the failed promise of the past (most clearly indicated in the banking position he "lost") has left him with no philosophical position with which he can compromise or in any way mitigate the present. Asking no quarter from the world, he can receive none.

One might find it hard to accept that Faulkner, Thomas Wolfe, or, a bit later, Robert Penn Warren was concerned with the same world as Hemingway or Fitzgerald. Yet these archetypes—the inchoate southerner lost in a world of the past, the occultist romantic who cannot reconcile the ideal with the actual, the venal product of the New South, and the bitch-goddess—are hardly unique to Faulkner. They have their antecedents in the work of predecessors—in George W. Cable, in T. S. Stribling, in Ellen Glasgow, and in a host of antebellum and modern southern writers. And Faulkner's finest visions, *The Sound and the Fury, Absalom, Absalom!,* and *Light in August,* are certainly much more than thinly disguised allegories of the struggle of the South with the exigencies of the new century (though there is no dearth of critics who have pointed out these allegorical elements). Although these novels are in a large sense psychological, they are not, at heart, novels about psychology (as another critical vogue has belabored them). Nor are they Faulkner's attempt at a *Ulysses* in a southern setting, though certainly the influence of Joyce (and of Conrad and other Continental writers) is evident throughout Faulkner's work. Nor, I believe, are these works Faulkner's reply to the challenge posed by the Canadian Shreve McCannon in *Absalom, Absalom!* to "Tell about the South. What it's like there. What do they do there. Why do they live there. Why do they live at all."

Rather, these novels are a result of the same authorial motivation that links Faulkner with the equally famous midwestern writer Ernest Hemingway. And that motivation is to answer, in their own regionally influenced voices, the question that Sartre articulates for the artist: How do we make sense of the world that we see? That the answers could be so very different, and yet the intellectual despair so similar, points out clearly the role of region both in philosophy and in form. Though it is perhaps too simply put, the assumptions behind the work of Hemingway and Faulkner are again the separate literary ways of viewing the world—the realistic and the romantic. Only this time the reflexive use of the genre that began with Glasgow and Cather finds yet another reversal in Faulkner and Hemingway. Certainly Faulkner's southern gestalt is romantic and Hemingway's bleak minimalist world realistic. Faulkner's Compsons and McCaslins, Hightowers and Sutpens are haunted by ghosts of the past, by the epic stories that they can only emulate and never fully achieve. And certainly Hemingway's modern disillusionists, Jake Barnes, Brett Ashley, Robert Jordan, and Frederic Henry, are forced, eyelids open, to confront the world that is *seen* rather than the world that is *felt*. But the despair of the worldviews is the same. Faulkner's Joe Christmas explains, "All I wanted was peace, it don't seem too much to ask," and Hemingway's Jake Barnes responds, "Isn't it pretty to think so?"

At heart, the movement in Glasgow's work from the romantic to the realistic is the movement also of Faulkner's novelistic necessity—namely, that no matter how lamentable, the past must be reinterpreted in the present. This is seen, for example, in Hightower's movement in *Light in August* from the decay of his house into the world of action to bring in a new life (Lena's child) and to attempt to save another, even a Joe Christmas.

And for Hemingway, the tendency inherited from Cather to escape from the real into the romantic is clearly evinced in the romantic stoics of *The Sun Also Rises, A Farewell to Arms,* and *For Whom the Bell Tolls.* For these are the characters who know better than to believe in those Faulknerian abstractions of honor, pity, courage, compassion, sacrifice, and love. They are doomed to believe in what they see, and yet often what they see is only the outward extension of what they feel. Pedro Romero, the bullfighter in *The Sun Also Rises,* is really an abstraction, someone to be preciously guarded against corruption, and who, faced with the modern world, is corruptible. And yet, although few of the characters of Faulkner's greatest work ever successfully achieve or develop into the ideals of his litanies, often they are destroyed by the failure of these abstractions to coalesce and make the modern world meaningful. Hemingway's characters, on the other hand, seem to leap into a world of regretful absolutes that they are constantly denying. Brett and Jake are true lovers caught in the absolute agony of Dante's Paolo and Francesca, doomed to "love that does not absolve the loved from loving." They are two survivors of "that dirty war" who aspire to deny all they have learned. Romantically, Robert Jordan has the opportunity to reflect on his love and courage as he waits with broken leg to immolate himself upon the altar of honor and duty in *For Whom the Bell Tolls*. In the final scenes of *A Farewell to Arms* all of nature cries with Frederic Henry as he walks home in the rain following Catherine Barkley's death in childbirth.

Implicit, however, in any discussion of these two writers is the nature of what *is* for each writer, as opposed to what only *seems to be*. Hemingway's universe is governed by the simplicity and paradoxical complexity of Gertrude Stein's famous statement that "a rose is a rose is a rose is a rose." His is a world that distrusts Faulkner's absolutes and their rendering into language. In "The Short Happy Life of Francis Macomber," Wilson the great white hunter warns his protégé Macomber not to talk about courage because it "doesn't do to talk too much about all this. Talk the whole thing away. No pleasure in anything if you mouth it up too much." Frederic Henry acknowledges a similar distrust of language in *A Farewell to Arms:*

> I was always embarrassed by the words sacred, glorious, and sacrifice and the expression in vain. We had heard them, sometimes standing in the rain almost out of earshot, so that only the shouted words came through, and had read them, on proclamations that were slapped up by billposters over other proclamations, now for a long time, and I had seen nothing sacred, and the things that were glorious had no glory and the sacrifices were like the stockyards at Chicago if nothing was done with the meat except to bury it. There were many words that you could not stand to hear and finally only the names of places had dignity. Certain numbers were the same way and certain dates and these with the names of the places were all you could say and have them mean anything. Abstract

words such as glory, honor, courage, or hallow were obscene beside the concrete names of villages, the numbers of roads, the names of rivers, the numbers of regiments and the dates.

Yet what Hemingway seemingly abhors, Faulkner celebrates. In *Absalom, Absalom!,* those weary young (and doomed) Confederates, Charles Bon and Henry Sutpen, find the absolutes worth dying for. Yet Hemingway's distrust of the absolutes produces the same results in the particular. Robert Jordan, hardened cynic that he is, is in his final actions not so far removed from the romantic protagonist of *A Tale of Two Cities,* who does "a far, far better thing . . . than I have ever done." Jordan dies for the particular, but the universal values are the same: like Charles Bon and Henry Sutpen, he dies for a cause desperately lost.

Allen Tate's credo of honor in "Ode to the Confederate Dead":

You who have waited for the angry resolution
Of those desires that should be yours tomorrow,
You know the unimportant shrift of death
And praise the vision
And praise the arrogant circumstance
Of those who fall
Rank upon rank, hurried beyond decision—
Here by the sagging gate, stopped by the wall.

is met with Hemingway's cynical ditty "The age demanded that we dance / and jammed us into iron pants." Tate's and Hemingway's reactions are apparently to the same demand, but they are expressed from a different formula for what the world is and what it means. The differences, I would maintain, are strictly regional.

Bibliography

Anderson, David D. "The Dimensions of the Midwest." *MidAmerica*, I (1974), 7–15.

———. "Notes Toward a Definition of the Mind of the Midwest." *MidAmerica*, III (1976), 7–16.

Atherton, Lewis. *Main Street on the Middle Border*. Bloomington, 1954.

Auchincloss, Louis. *Pioneers & Caretakers: A Study of Nine American Women Novelists*. Minneapolis, 1965.

Barzun, Jacques. *Romanticism and the Modern Ego*. Boston, 1943.

Becker, George J., ed. *Documents of Modern Literary Realism*. Princeton, 1963.

Bell, Michael Davitt. *The Development of American Romance: The Sacrifice of Relation*. Chicago, 1980.

Billington, Ray Allen. "The Garden of the World: Fact and Fiction." In *The Heritage of the Middle West*, edited by John J. Murray. Norman, Okla., 1958.

Bromfield, Louis. *The Green Bay Tree*. New York, 1924.

Brooks, Van Wyck. *America's Coming-of-Age*. New York, 1915.

———. *The Confident Years: 1885–1915*. New York, 1952.

———. "On Creating a Usable Past." *The Dial*. April 11, 1918, pp. 337–41.

Brown, E. K., and Leon Edel. *Willa Cather: A Critical Biography*. New York, 1953.

Bryer, Jackson R., ed. *Fifteen Modern American Authors: A Survey of Research and Criticism.* Durham, 1969.

Butcher, Philip. *George Washington Cable.* New York, 1962.

Cable, George W. *The Grandissimes: A Story of Creole Life.* 1880; rpr. New York, 1957.

Carter, Everett. *Howells and the Age of Realism.* Philadelphia, 1950.

Cash, W. J. *The Mind of the South.* New York, 1941.

Cather, Willa. *My Ántonia.* Boston, 1918.

————. "The Novel Démeublé." In *Not Under Forty.* New York, 1936.

————. *O Pioneers!* Boston, 1913.

————. *The Professor's House.* New York, 1925.

Chase, Richard. *The American Novel and Its Tradition.* Garden City, N.Y., 1957.

Clark, William Bedford. "Humor in Cable's *The Grandissimes.*" *Southern Quarterly: A Journal of the Arts in the South,* XVIII (Summer, 1980), 51–59.

Clemens, Samuel L. *Life on the Mississippi.* 1874; rpr. New York, 1968.

Collingwood, R. G. "The Historical Imagination." In *The Idea of History.* 1946; rpr. New York, 1993.

Cooper, James Fenimore. *Notions of the Americans: Picked up by a Travelling Bachelor.* Vol. II of 2 vols. Philadelphia, 1828.

Cowie, Alexander. *The Rise of the American Novel.* New York, 1948.

————, ed. "The Yemassee Uprising." In *The Yemassee,* by William Gilmore Simms. New York, 1962.

Dabbs, James McBride. *Who Speaks for the South?* New York, 1964.

Davidson, Donald. *The Attack on Leviathan: Regionalism and Nationalism in the United States.* Chapel Hill, 1938.

————. *"Still Rebels, Still Yankees" and Other Essays.* Baton Rouge, 1957.

Dondore, Dorothy Anne. *The Prairie and the Making of Middle America: Four Centuries of Description.* Cedar Rapids, Iowa, 1926.

Duffey, Bernard I. "Hamlin Garland's 'Decline' from Realism." *American Literature,* XV (1953), 69–74.

Eaton, Richard Bozman. "George W. Cable and the Historical Romance." *Southern Literary Journal,* VIII (Fall, 1975), 82–94.

Eggleston, Edward. *The Hoosier School-Master.* Library Edition. New York, 1892.

Faulkner, William. *Absalom, Absalom!* New York, 1936.

————. *Intruder in the Dust.* New York, 1948.

————. *Light in August.* New York, 1932.

————. *The Sound and the Fury.* New York, 1929.

Fitzgerald, F. Scott. *The Great Gatsby.* New York, 1925.

Flanagan, John T. "Joseph Kirkland, Pioneer Realist." *American Literature,* XI (1939), 273–84.

————. Introduction to *Zury: The Meanest Man in Spring County*, by Edgar Watson Howe. 1887; rpr. Urbana, 1956.

Foote, Shelby. *The Civil War: A Narrative.* Vol. III of 3 vols. New York, 1974.

Frost, Robert. "The Gift Outright," in *The Poetry of Robert Frost.* New York, 1970.

Frye, Northrop. *Anatomy of Criticism: Four Essays.* Princeton, 1957.

Fussell, Edwin. *Frontier: American Literature and the American West.* Princeton, 1965.

Fussell, Paul. *The Great War and Modern Memory.* New York, 1975.

Garland, Hamlin. *Crumbling Idols: Twelve Essays on Art Dealing Chiefly with Literature, Painting, and the Drama.* Edited by Jane Johnson. 1894; rpr. Cambridge, Mass., 1960.

————. *Main-Travelled Roads.* Introduction by William Dean Howells. 1891; rpr. New York, 1899.

————. *Rose of Dutcher's Coolly.* Chicago, 1895.

————. *A Son of the Middle Border.* New York, 1917.

Gerber, Philip. *Willa Cather.* Boston, 1975.

Ginger, Ray. *Altgeld's America: The Lincoln Ideal Versus Changing Realities.* New York, 1958.

Glasgow, Ellen. *Barren Ground.* Garden City, N.Y., 1925.

————. *The Battle-Ground.* New York, 1902.

————. *A Certain Measure: An Interpretation of Prose Fiction.* New York, 1943.

————. *The Woman Within.* New York, 1954.

Godbold, E. Stanly, Jr. *Ellen Glasgow and the Woman Within.* Baton Rouge, 1972.

Grant, Ulysses S. *Personal Memoirs of U. S. Grant.* New York, 1886.

Gray, Richard. *The Literature of Memory: Modern Writers of the American South.* Baltimore, 1977.

Havighurst, Walter, ed. *Land of the Long Horizons.* New York, 1960.

Hawthorne, Nathaniel. *The House of the Seven Gables.* Columbus, Ohio, 1965. Edited by William Charvat, Roy Harvey Pearce, and Claude M. Simpson. Vol II of *The Centenary Edition of the Works of Nathaniel Hawthorne.*

————. *The Marble Faun; or, The Romance of Monte Beni.* Columbus, Ohio, 1968. Edited by William Charvat *et al.* Vol. IV of *The Centenary Edition of the Works of Nathaniel Hawthorne.*

Hemingway, Ernest. *A Farewell to Arms.* New York, 1929.

————. *For Whom the Bell Tolls.* New York, 1940.

————. *The Short Stories of Ernest Hemingway.* New York, 1966.

————. *The Sun Also Rises.* New York, 1926.

Henderson, Harry B. *Versions of the Past: The Historical Imagination in American Fiction.* New York, 1974.

Henson, Clyde E. "Joseph Kirkland's Influence on Hamlin Garland," *American Literature,* XXIII (1952), 459–63.

Herron, Ima. *The Small Town in American Literature.* Durham, 1939.

Hicks, John D. "A Political Whirlpool." In *The Heritage of the Middle West,* edited by John J. Murray. Norman, Okla., 1958.

Hilfer, Anthony Channell. *The Revolt from the Village, 1915–1930.* Chapel Hill, 1969.

Hinz, Evelyn J. "Willa Cather's Technique and the Ideology of Populism." *Western American Literature,* VII (1972), 47–61.

Hoffman, Frederick J. *The Twenties.* Rev. ed. New York, 1962.

Holman, C. Hugh. "Ellen Glasgow and the Southern Literary Tradition." In *Southern Writers: Appraisals in Our Time,* edited by R. C. Simonini, Jr. Charlottesville, 1964.

————. *The Immoderate Past: The Southern Writer and History.* Athens, Ga., 1977.

————. *The Roots of Southern Writing: Essays on the Literature of the American South.* Athens, Ga., 1972.

————, ed. Introduction to *The Yemassee,* by William Gilmore Simms. Boston, 1961.

Howe, E. W. *The Story of a Country Town.* Edited by Claude M. Simpson. Cambridge, Mass., 1961.

Howells, William Dean. *"Criticism and Fiction" and Other Essays.* Edited by Clara Marburg Kirk and Rudolf Kirk. New York, 1959.

————. Introduction to *Main-Travelled Roads,* by Hamlin Garland. 1891; rpr. New York, 1899.

Hubbell, Jay B. *South and Southwest: Literary Essays and Reminiscences.* Durham, 1965.

————. *The South in American Literature, 1607–1900.* Durham, 1954.

Hutton, Graham. *Midwest at Noon.* Chicago, 1946.

Inge, M. Thomas, ed. *Ellen Glasgow: Centennial Essays.* Charlottesville, 1976.

Jensen, Merrill, ed. *Regionalism in America.* Madison, 1951.

Jones, Howard Mumford. *The Age of Energy: Varieties of American Experience, 1865–1915.* New York, 1971.

————. *The Theory of American Literature.* Ithaca, 1948.

Kazin, Alfred. *On Native Grounds: An Interpretation of Modern American Prose Literature.* New York, 1942.

Kennedy, John Pendleton. *Swallow Barn; or, A Sojourn in the Old Dominion.* Introduction and notes by William S. Osborne. 1832; rpr. of 1853 ed., New York, 1962.

Kirkland, Caroline Matilda. *Forest Life.* Vol. II of 2 vols. New York, 1842.

————. *A New Home—Who'll Follow? or, Glimpses of Western Life.* Edited by Sandra A. Zagarell. New Brunswick, N.J., 1990.

————. "Periodical Reading." *United States Magazine and Democratic Review,* XVI (January, 1845), 61.

Kirkland, Joseph. *Zury: The Meanest Man in Spring County.* Introduction by John T. Flanagan. 1887; rpr. Urbana, 1956.

Lawrence, D. H. *Studies in Classic American Literature.* New York, 1923.

Lease, Benjamin. "Realism and Joseph Kirkland's *Zury.*" *American Literature,* XXIII (1952), 464–66.

Lee, Robert Edson. *From West to East: Studies in the Literature of the American West.* Urbana, 1966.

Leisy, Ernest E. *The American Historical Novel.* Norman, Okla., 1950.

Lewis, R. W. B. *The American Adam: Innocence, Tragedy, and Tradition in the Nineteenth Century.* Chicago, 1955.

Lively, Robert A. *Fiction Fights the Civil War: An Unfinished Chapter in the Literary History of the American People.* Chapel Hill, 1957.

Lukács, Georg. *The Historical Novel.* Translated by Hannah Mitchell and Stanley Mitchell. Boston, 1963.

————. *Realism in Our Time: Literature and the Class Struggle.* Translated by John Mander and Necke Mander. Edited by Ruth Nanda Anshen. New York, 1964.

McAvoy, Thomas T., *et al. The Midwest: Myth or Reality?* Notre Dame, 1961.

McCloskey, John C. "Jacksonian Democracy in Mrs. Kirkland's *A New Home—Who'll Follow?*" *Michigan History,* XLV (December, 1961), 347–52.

McCullough, Joseph B. *Hamlin Garland.* Boston, 1978.

McDowell, Frederick P. W. *Ellen Glasgow and the Ironic Art of Fiction.* Madison, 1960.

Martin, Jay. *Harvests of Change: American Literature, 1865–1914.* Englewood Cliffs, N.J., 1967.

Marx, Leo. *The Machine in the Garden: Technology and the Pastoral Ideal in America.* New York, 1964.

Meyer, Roy W. *The Middle Western Farm Novel in the Twentieth Century.* Lincoln, 1965.

Miller, Charles T. "Hamlin Garland's Retreat from Realism." *Western American Literature,* I (1966), 119–29.

Nemanic, Gerald, ed. *A Bibliographical Guide to Midwestern Literature.* Iowa City, 1981.

Nye, Russel B. *Midwestern Progressive Politics: A Historical Study of Its Origins and Development, 1870–1950.* East Lansing, 1951.

O'Brien, Michael. *The Idea of the American South, 1920–1941.* Baltimore, 1979.

O'Connor, Flannery. "The Fiction Writer & His Country." In *Mystery and Manners: Occasional Prose,* edited by Sally Fitzgerald and Robert Fitzgerald. New York, 1969.

Odum, Howard W., and Harry Estill Moore. *American Regionalism: A Cultural-Historical Approach to National Integration.* New York, 1938.

Olson, Charles. *Call Me Ishmael.* New York, 1947.

Osborne, William S., ed. Introduction to *A New Home—Who'll Follow?,* by Caroline Matilda Kirkland. New Haven, 1965.

————, ed. Introduction to *Swallow Barn; or, A Sojourn in the Old Dominion,* by John Pendleton Kennedy. Hafner Library of Classics. 1832; rpr. of 1853 ed., New York, 1962.

Parrington, Vernon Louis, Jr. *The Romantic Revolution in America.* New York, 1958. Vol. II of *Main Currents in American Thought: An Interpretation of American Literature from the Beginnings to 1920.*

Pizer, Donald. *Hamlin Garland's Early Work and Career.* Berkeley, 1960.

Porte, Joel. *The Romance in America: Studies in Cooper, Poe, Hawthorne, Melville, and James.* Middletown, Conn., 1969.

Randall, John H., III. "Interpretation of *My Ántonia.*" In *Willa Cather and Her Critics,* edited by James Schroeter. Ithaca, 1967.

Raper, J. R. *Without Shelter: The Early Career of Ellen Glasgow.* Baton Rouge, 1971.

Richardson, Thomas J., ed. "Centennial Essays: George W. Cable's *The Grandissimes.*" *Southern Quarterly,* XVIII (Summer, 1980).

Ridgely, J. V. *John Pendleton Kennedy.* New York, 1966.

————. *William Gilmore Simms.* New York, 1962.

Rouse, Blair. *Ellen Glasgow.* New York, 1962.

Rubin, Louis D., Jr. *George W. Cable: The Life and Times of a Southern Heretic.* New York, 1969.

————. "The Image of an Army: The Civil War in Southern Fiction." In *Southern Writers: Appraisals in Our Time,* edited by R. C. Simonini, Jr. Charlottesville, 1964.

————, ed. *A Bibliographical Guide to the Study of Southern Literature.* Baton Rouge, 1969.

Rubin, Louis D., Jr., and C. Hugh Holman, eds. *Southern Literary Study: Problems and Possibilities.* Chapel Hill, 1975.

Ruland, Richard. *The Rediscovery of American Literature: Premises of Critical Taste, 1900–1940.* Cambridge, Mass., 1967.

Santas, Joan Foster. *Ellen Glasgow's American Dream.* Charlottesville, 1965.

Scholes, Robert, and Robert Kellogg. *The Nature of Narrative.* New York, 1966.

Schroeter, James, ed. *Willa Cather and Her Critics*. Ithaca, 1967.

Sellers, Charles Grier, Jr., ed. *The Southerner As American*. Chapel Hill, 1960.

Sergeant, Elizabeth Shepley. *Willa Cather: A Memoir*. Philadelphia, 1953.

Sharp, Paul. "From Poverty to Prosperity." In *The Heritage of the Middle West*, edited by John J. Murray. Norman, Okla., 1958.

Sherman, William T. *Memoirs of General William T. Sherman*. Vol. II of 2 vols. New York, 1875.

Simms, William Gilmore. *The Letters of William Gilmore Simms*. Vol. I of 5 vols. Edited by Mary C. Simms Oliphant, Alfred Taylor Odell, and T. C. Duncan Eaves. Columbia, S.C., 1952.

———. *Views and Reviews in American Literature, History, and Fiction*. Edited by C. Hugh Holman. Cambridge, Mass., 1962.

———. *The Wigwam and the Cabin*. New York, 1882.

———. *The Yemassee*. Edited by Alexander Cowie. New York, 1962.

Simpson, Claude M., ed. Introduction to *The Story of a Country Town*, by Edgar Watson Howe. Cambridge, Mass., 1961.

Slote, Bernice. "Willa Cather." In *Fifteen Modern American Authors: A Survey of Research and Criticism*, edited by Jackson R. Bryer. Durham, 1969.

Slote, Bernice, and Virginia Faulkner, eds. *The Art of Willa Cather*. Lincoln, 1974.

Smith, Henry Nash. *Virgin Land: The American West as Symbol and Myth*. Cambridge, Mass., 1950.

Spencer, Benjamin T. *The Quest for Nationality: An American Literary Campaign*. Syracuse, 1957.

Stewart, Randall. "Hawthorne's Contributions to *The Salem Advertiser*." *American Literature*, V (1934), 327–41.

———. *Regionalism and Beyond: Essays of Randall Stewart*. Edited by George Core. Nashville, 1968.

Tate, Allen. *Collected Poems, 1919–1976*. New York, 1977.

———. *Essays of Four Decades*. Chicago. 1968.

Taylor, William R. *Cavalier and Yankee: The Old South and American National Character*. New York, 1961.

Turner, Arlin. *George W. Cable: A Biography*. Durham, 1956.

Turner, Frederick Jackson. *The Frontier in American History*. New York, 1920.

Twelve Southerners. *I'll Take My Stand: The South and the Agrarian Tradition*. New York, 1930.

Van Doren, Carl. *The American Novel: 1789–1939*. New York, 1940.

Van Ghent, Dorothy. *Willa Cather*. Minneapolis, 1964.

Wagenknecht, Edward. *Cavalcade of the American Novel: From the Birth of the Nation to the Middle of the Twentieth Century*. New York, 1952.

Walcutt, Charles Child. *American Literary Naturalism: A Divided Stream.* Minneapolis, 1956.

Warren, Robert Penn. *Jefferson Davis Gets His Citizenship Back.* Lexington, Ky., 1980.

Watson, Craig. "I'll Take My Flight: The Village Lost and Found." In "Habit of Mind: Studies in the Literature of the Middle West of the Twentieth Century." Ph.D. dissertation, University of Michigan, 1980.

Williams, Stanley T. "Nathaniel Hawthorne." In *Literary History of the United States.* Vol. I of 3 vols., edited by Robert E. Spiller *et al.* New York, 1974.

Wilson, Edmund. *Patriotic Gore: Studies in the Literature of the American Civil War.* New York, 1962.

Woodress, James. *Willa Cather: Her Life and Art.* New York, 1970.

Woodward, C. Vann. *The Burden of Southern History.* Baton Rouge, 1960.

Ziff, Larzer. *The American 1890s: Life and Times of a Lost Generation.* New York, 1966.

Index

Farewell to Arms, A (Hemingway), 83,
    120–22
Faulkner, William, 5, 11, 13, 15, 18,
    20–22, 61, 87, 110ff., 116ff.
Fitzgerald, F. Scott, 5, 15, 20, 52,
    110ff., 119ff.
Fitzhugh, George, 41
Flaubert, Gustave, 49
Fletcher, John Gould, 20*n*
Flush Times (Hooper), 71
Foote, Shelby, 7–8
For Whom the Bell Tolls (Hemingway),
    120, 121
Forayers, The (Simms), 81
Forest Life (Kirkland), 54–55
Franklin, Benjamin, 16
Frederic, Harold, 79
Free silver movement, 51
Freud, Sigmund, 114
Frontier, 9, 25ff., 35, 45, 54–55, 71
Frost, Robert, 36
Fussell, Paul, 113

Garland, Hamlin, 12–13, 28, 30, 50,
    55, 64, 66–68, 74ff., 85*n*, 91–92,
    97–98, 109, 110
—works: *Crumbling Idols*, 12–13, 28,
    30, 75ff., 110; *Main-Travelled Roads*,
    67–68, 74ff., 91–92; *Rose of Dutch-
    er's Coolly*, 79*n*, 97; *A Son of the
    Middle Border*, 74*n*
George W. Cable (Rubin), 84
George, Henry, 76
Gettysburg, battle of, 92
Giants in the Earth (Rölvaag), 19, 67
"Gift Outright, The"(Frost), 36
Glasgow, Ellen, 20, 81–97, 107ff.,
    117, 119
—works: *Barren Ground*, 20, 87,
    93ff., 107ff.; *The Battle-Ground*,
    86ff., 108ff.; *A Certain Measure*,
    82–97 passim; *The Deliverance*, 87,
    92–93; *The Descendant*, 88; *In This*

Our Life, 87*n*; *The Miller of Old
    Church*, 87–88; *Phases of an Inferior
    Planet*, 88; *The Sheltered Life*, 87*n*;
    They Stooped to Folly, 87*n*; *The
    Voice of the People*, 88; *The Woman
    Within*, 91, 110
"Go Down, Moses" (Faulkner), 61
Gone with the Wind (Mitchell), 83
Grandissimes, The (Cable), 84ff.
Granger movement, 51
Grant, Ulysses S., 7–9, 16, 24
Great Gatsby, The (Fitzgerald), 16, 20,
    52
Great War and Modern Memory, The
    (Fussell), 113
Green Bay Tree, The (Bromfield), 18–
    19
Guy Rivers (Simms), 81*n*

Hall, Captain Basil, 52, 53
Harper's Magazine, 79
Hawthorne, Nathaniel, 25–48, 58,
    110
Haymarket Square bombing, 8
Hegel, G. W. F., 114
Hemingway, Ernest, 5, 16, 83, 110ff.,
    116, 118ff.
Henry St. John, Gentleman (Cooke),
    82
Hilfer, Anthony, 65*n*, 73, 97–98
Hilt to Hilt (Cooke), 82
History of Southern Literature, The
    (Rubin), 4
Hoffman, Charles Fenno, 52
Holman, C. Hugh, 1–4, 6, 31
Hooper, Johnson Jones, 71
Hoosier School-Master, The (Eggleston),
    14, 50, 64ff., 76
Horse-Shoe Robinson (Kennedy), 82
House of the Seven Gables, The (Haw-
    thorne), 31, 34
Howe, E. W., 50, 55, 64, 67ff., 76,
    97–98, 109

Howells, William Dean, 49, 70, 76, 78, 87, 115
Hubbell, Jay B., 59*n*, 60*n*
Huysmans, J. K., 49
Hyperion (Longfellow), 58

I'll Take My Stand (Twelve Southerners), 10ff., 20
Immoderate Past, The (Holman), 83
In Ole Virginia (Page), 83
In This Our Life (Glasgow), 87*n*
Indians, 29ff.
International theme, 33ff.
Intruder in the Dust (Faulkner), 18ff.
Irving, Washington, 21, 53, 58, 59

Jackson, Andrew, 41, 51
James, Henry, 34, 36, 49–50
Jefferson Davis Gets His Citizenship Back (Warren), 19
Jefferson, Thomas, 16, 21, 23
John March, Southerner (Cable), 85
Jones, Howard Mumford, 22
Joyce, James, 113, 114
Jung, Carl, 114

Katharine Walton (Simms), 81
Kazin, Alfred, 109
Kellogg, Robert, 40
Kennedy, John Pendleton, 58ff., 82–83, 110
"Kentucky Tragedy," 82*n*
Kinsmen, The (Simms). See *Scout, The* (Simms)
Kirkland, Caroline, 50, 52ff., 63ff., 70, 80, 110
Kirkland, Joseph, 50, 64, 67ff., 76, 79, 109
Kline, Henry Blue, 20*n*

Lanier, Lyle H., 20*n*
Last of the Mohicans, The (Cooper), 30*n*

Lawrence, D. H., 46
Leather Stocking and Silk (Cooke), 82
Leatherstocking Tales (Cooper), 26, 29ff., 46, 58
Lee, Robert E., 7–9, 16, 24
Lewis, R. W. B., 23
Lewis, Sinclair, 16, 20, 55, 80, 96, 109, 111
Lewis, Wyndham, 111
Lexington, Mass., battle of, 8
Life on the Mississippi (Twain), 54
Light in August (Faulkner), 119ff.
Lincoln, Abraham, 51
Lincoln, Nebr., 98, 102, 103
Lively, Robert A., 83*n*
Local color literature, 14, 84ff.
Longfellow, Henry W., 58
Louisiana Purchase, 84
Lowell, James Russell, 65
Lytle, Andrew, 11*n*, 20*n*

Machine in the Garden, The (Marx), 23
Main Currents in American Thought (Parrington), 27, 40
Main Street (Lewis), 98
Main-Travelled Roads (Garland), 67–68, 74ff., 91–92
Marble Faun, The (Hawthorne), 27–28, 33–34
Marx, Leo, 23
Matthiessen, F. O., 32
McCullers, Carson, 20
"Mediterranean, The" (Tate), 41*n*
Mellichampe (Simms), 32, 81
Melville, Herman, 36
Memoirs (Sherman), 9
Middle Border, 49, 50ff., 67ff.
Miller of Old Church, The (Glasgow), 87–88
Mind of the South, The (Cash), 17
Miss Ravenel's Conversion (DeForest), 83